W9-BRH-696

AN INSTANT GUIDE TO

SEASHELLS

The most familiar species of
North American seashells
described and illustrated in color

Pamela Forey and Cecilia Fitzsimons

BONANZA BOOKS
New York

First published 1987 by Bonanza Books,
distributed by Crown Publishers, Inc.

© 1987 Atlantis Publications Ltd.

Printed in Spain by Sirven Grafic

D.L. B.1927-1990

ISBN: 0-517-63548-8

Contents

INTRODUCTION   8

HOW TO USE THIS BOOK   8

GUIDE TO IDENTIFICATION   8

GLOSSARY OF TERMS   12

GASTROPOD SHELLS   14

BIVALVE SHELLS   80

CHITONS   120

TUSK SHELLS   121

INDEX AND CHECKLIST   122

Introduction

Seashells belong to the group of animals called molluscs. Many live in the shallow offshore waters along our coasts and others live in the intertidal zone. Most of them produce shells that protect them from predators and those that live on the shore are also protected by their shells from surf and desiccation. When the animals die, their shells remain for long afterwards and may even be fossilized. The beaches are good places to look for seashells, for as well as those that live on the shore there are often dead shells of offshore animals that have been washed onto the beach.

This book will help identify the shells that you find on the beach, or see in gift shops at the coast, or even that you eat at a clam bake. We have selected from the several thousands of N. American seashells those species most widely distributed along our coastlines and in the Caribbean, and the shells most likely to be encountered by visitors to the coast.

How to use this book

The book is divided into four sections of molluscs, based on the form of their shells. The sections are *Gastropod Shells*, *Bivalve Shells*, *Chitons* and *Tusk Shells*. Each section is indicated by a different color band at the top of the page. To identify your shell, first decide to which section it belongs, using the information and symbols in the *Guide to Identification* which follows. It is possible that you will not be able to find your exact shell in this book for there are thousands of seashells on our coasts. However we have included many of the familiar shells as well as examples of the major families and genera, so that you should be able to find one similar if not the same. There are many species found on the coasts of California and Baja California that are not found elsewhere, far too many to include in a book of this size. Therefore for these areas we have included only a selection of the most common species. However, for every Californian species, there is often a more widely distributed, closely related eastern or western counterpart and so even for Californian species it will often be possible to find a similar species in the book.

Guide to identification

First decide to which section your shell belongs.

Gastropods   These animals have a single, large shell which may be spirally coiled, dome-shaped, cap-shaped or cone-shaped. Spirally coiled shells are usually twisted into a helix but some are coiled in a flat plane, and in others the helix opens out into an irregularly twisted form. The last whorl of the coil, the body whorl, is the largest, the one in which the animal lives. The shells may be simple and unadorned or may have complex decorations of spines and sculpturing.

Bivalves These animals have a shell consisting of two more or less equal valves, joined by a hinge. In life, the two valves are closed by powerful muscles, but after the animal has died the two valves often become separated or spread out.

Chitons Easily recognized by the eight, often overlapping, plates which make up the shell. They form a wide band along the back of the animal and are held in place by an encircling girdle. Chitons are usually found alive.

Tusk Shells These animals have hollow, tubular, tusk-like shells which are open at both ends. The shell tapers from the bottom to the top; in life the head of the animal emerges from the larger, bottom opening. Since they live in deep water, these animals are not usually seen alive but their empty shells are washed up onto beaches.

Making a positive identification

Within the first two sections shells are sequenced by size from the smallest to the largest, to enable you to find your particular shell easily. The size of each shell is given at the top of the page, together with a size symbol for easy reference (see Fig. 1). For most gastropods, the size refers to the height from the tip of the spire to the bottom of the shell; however in some shells, like abalones and limpets, it is the length of the shell which has been measured, and in some flattened shells the width has been given. This is indicated wherever relevant. For bivalves, chitons and tusk shells, the size refers to the length of the shell from the front to hind end.

By flicking through your section you can narrow down the field to seashells of a particular size. Also in the box at the top of the page you will find the occurrence of the shell (**E** for east coast, **W** for west coast and **C** for Caribbean); and the illustration and text contained in the four boxes enable you to make a positive identification.

Characteristic Features

The first two boxes are designed to be used together, to enable you to make a quick identification. The first box gives details which identify the shell as a particular species, as a Black Abalone for example, rather than any other kind of abalone. The second box provides other information of a more general nature, on the shape and form of the shell, height of spire, position of beaks etc., and which may be true of abalones as a whole for example, rather than just the Black Abalone. You can often use the second box to identify the type of shell you have

Fig. 1 Key to size symbols

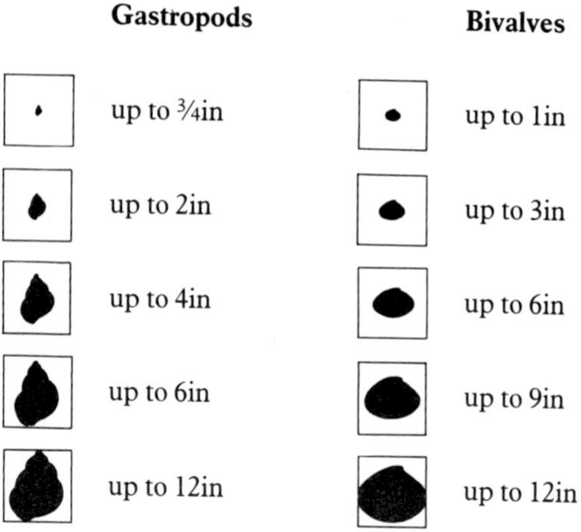

Gastropods		**Bivalves**	
·	up to ¾in	•	up to 1in
◗	up to 2in	●	up to 3in
◢	up to 4in	⬤	up to 6in
◣	up to 6in	⬤	up to 9in
◣	up to 12in	⬤	up to 12in

found, as an olive, for example, even if your particular olive is not the species illustrated.

In some cases the second box also contains information about the economic significance of the shell, its culinary use or its present population status due to past collection.

Habitat and Distribution

The habitat in which a shell is found and its distribution on our coastlines are important clues to its identity. The shells in this book fall into four basic distribution patterns: those found on the east coast (many of them north of N. Carolina); those found on the southeast coast, from N. Carolina southwards, and in the Caribbean; those found on the west coast from Alaska to California; and those found in California and Baja California. Most of the shells we have included come from the first three categories. The distribution of each shell is given in a map in the illustration and more detailed information on habitat and occurrence is given in the box.

Related and similar species

Finally, in the fourth box, are given some of the related or similar shells which are found on our coasts. Those species printed in **bold** type are illustrated, either as featured species or in the *Other Common Species* sections; those printed in ordinary type are not. Not all related or similar species have been mentioned since there are several thousand seashells on the coasts of North America. Those omitted are generally much less likely to be seen, either because they are local or rare; or because they live in deep water or bury themselves in mud; or because they are very small.

Other common species

At the end of the gastropod and bivalve sections you will find pages of other common species. These are mostly less common than the featured seashells or less obvious.

Now you are ready to use this book. It is designed to fit into your pocket, so take it with you on your next trip to the coast and don't forget to check your sightings on the check-list provided with the index. Looking for animals on a seashore is an exciting pastime, but please remember that these are living animals and leave them on the beach where they live. Hundreds of creatures live on the shore, many of them under rocks and stones, where they are protected from surf and desiccation; if you turn over the stones to look at what is beneath, please make sure you turn them back again so that the animals are not killed by sun or sea. Look for the dead shells cast up by the waves and take them home and photograph the others.

Fig. 2 Specimen page

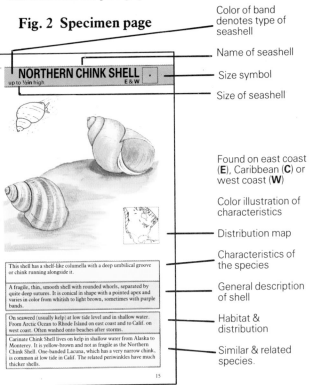

Color of band denotes type of seashell

Name of seashell

NORTHERN CHINK SHELL .
up to ½in high   E & W

Size symbol

Size of seashell

Found on east coast (**E**), Caribbean (**C**) or west coast (**W**)

Color illustration of characteristics

Distribution map

Characteristics of the species

This shell has a shelf-like columella with a deep umbilical groove or chink running alongside it.

A fragile, thin, smooth shell with rounded whorls, separated by quite deep sutures. It is conical in shape with a pointed apex and varies in color from whitish to light brown, sometimes with purple bands.

General description of shell

On seaweed (usually kelp) at low tide level and in shallow water. From Arctic Ocean to Rhode Island on east coast and to Calif. on west coast. Often washed onto beaches after storms.

Habitat & distribution

Carinate Chink Shell lives on kelp in shallow water from Alaska to Monterey. It is yellow-brown and not as fragile as the Northern Chink Shell. One-banded Lacuna, which has a very narrow chink, is common at low tide in Calif. The related periwinkles have much thicker shells.

Similar & related species.

15

Glossary of terms

Aperture The opening of the shell in a gastropod.

Apex The tip of the spire in a gastropod.

Axial ribs Ridges which run from the apex of the shell to the aperture in a gastropod; or from the beaks to the margin of the shell in a bivalve.

Beak The apex of the valve in a bivalve shell.

Byssus A cluster of hair-like threads found in some bivalves which anchor the animal to the substrate. Such animals have a byssal notch, a hole in the shell through which the byssus passes.

Callus A button-like structure, found at the end of the cord surrounding the umbilicus of some gastropods.

Columella The thick central axis of a gastropod shell. It often extends beyond the aperture and forms the siphonal canal. In many shells there are folds or ridges on the columella where it borders the aperture.

Cords Ridges which run spirally around the shell. Where they cross the axial ridges, nodes or beads may form.

Growth lines Lines in the shells of bivalves and gastropods that mark former stages of growth in the shell.

Inflated Used to describe the appearance of some bivalve shells which look as if they have been blown up like a balloon.

Ligament A brown horny structure which, together with the hinge, links the two valves together, in bivalves. It is usually found outside the hinge.

Mantle The covering of the living animal which lines and secretes the shell. In most molluscs it remains inside the shell but in some gastropods, like the cowries, it extends out and over the shell.

Muscle scar The round scar on the inside of a bivalve shell marking the position of attachment of the muscle which holds the valves closed.

Operculum A horny or calcareous plate which closes the aperture in many gastropods. It is attached to the foot of the animal.

Periostracum A shiny or fibrous covering to the shell which is found on many living gastropods and bivalves. It may be very thin or quite thick and is often a different color to the shell itself. The periostracum is often worn away in places, especially on dead shells.

Shoulder The flattened space found at the top of some whorls in some gastropods.

Siphonal canal A channel at the base of the aperture in gastropods, through which the siphon protrudes in the living animal. The siphon is an extension of the mantle which carries water in and out of the shell.

Spire The whorls above the body whorl in a gastropod.

Suture The line between one whorl and the next.

Threads Small thread-like ridges which run spirally around the shell.

Umbilicus A hole found in some gastropods, at the base of the columella, formed because the whorls do not touch each at the base of the shell.

Valve One of the two halves of the shell in bivalves. The valves are connected together along the upper margin by a toothed hinge and ligament.

Varix (pl. varices) A large axial ridge found in some gastropods, for example murexes, which represents the former position of the outer lip of the aperture. It may bear spines or other decoration.

Whorl One turn of the shell in a gastropod. The body whorl is the lowermost and largest.

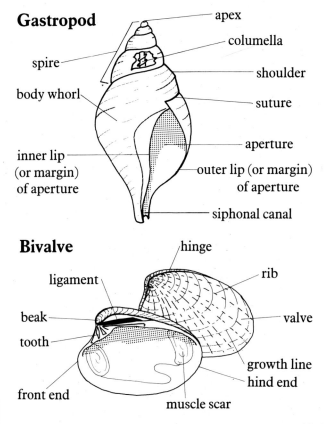

Gastropod

apex

columella

spire

shoulder

body whorl

suture

aperture

inner lip (or margin) of aperture

outer lip (or margin) of aperture

siphonal canal

Bivalve

hinge

ligament

rib

beak

valve

tooth

growth line

hind end

front end

muscle scar

Whitish or yellowish, body whorl often with three diffuse bands of darker color and tiny central whorl of spire also dark. Four red-brown spots occur on outer lip of aperture.

A smooth, shining shell with a very large body whorl and a low spire. The long narrow aperture has a short broad siphonal canal and white interior. Outer lip of aperture is smooth and thickened and the base of the columella has four spiral ridges.

In sand, amongst sea grasses in very shallow water. The mantle covers most of the shell in life. N. Carolina to Florida, the Gulf states and the West Indies.

Many margin shells live in shallow waters off the east coast and in the Caribbean. Some are minute, like Golden-lined and Teardrop Margin Shells, only ⅛in high. Others are larger, like Orange Margin Shell which grows up to ¾in high, and the elongated Oat Grain Margin Shell.

NORTHERN CHINK SHELL

up to ½in high

E & W

This shell has a shelf-like columella with a deep umbilical groove or chink running alongside it.

A fragile, thin, smooth shell with rounded whorls, separated by quite deep sutures. It is conical in shape with a pointed apex and varies in color from whitish to light brown, sometimes with purple bands.

On seaweed (usually kelp) at low tide level and in shallow water. From Arctic Ocean to Rhode Island on east coast and to Calif. on west coast. Often washed onto beaches after storms.

Carinate Chink Shell lives on kelp in shallow water from Alaska to Monterey. It is yellow-brown and not as fragile as the Northern Chink Shell. One-banded Lacuna, which has a very narrow chink, is common at low tide in Calif. The related periwinkles have much thicker shells.

15

White shell with 10–18 axial ribs on each whorl. The ribs end above and below the suture line, leaving a smooth band between the whorls.

An elongated shell with a high pointed spire. The aperture is ovate, rounded at its lower end.

Shallow and deep water from Alaska to San Diego, Calif. Turbonilles are external parasites on other shells and worms and are found on these animals.

Many similar turbonilles live on the west coast; they vary in color from white to yellow or brown. Some live on the shore, others in deep water. Others live off the east coast and in the Caribbean. The yellow Interrupted Turbonille lives in shallow water from the Gulf of St Lawrence to the West Indies.

16

Grayish or reddish brown shell with spirally arranged pairs of white knobs on spire whorls, and spiral threads on body whorl below knobs.

An elongated, spindle-shaped shell with a high pointed spire. Aperture ovate with a broad siphonal canal at the base and a notch at the top.

Intertidal zone and shallow water, near rubble and eelgrass; they live in colonies and prey on other animals using their poisonous teeth. Southern Florida, Texas and West Indies.

Many other small brown or black drillias are found in the Caribbean and the southern Pacific. They vary in distribution, habitat, size and decoration on the spire; examples include Cuban Drillia, White-banded Drillia and Oyster Drillia. Others are white or pink, like the Rough Drillia.

17

This white shell has many rugged, concentric ridges giving it a laminated appearance.

A heavy, thick, cap-shaped shell, variable in shape and with a poorly developed spire, either at one end or near the middle. The spire is often curved over to one side. The animal sits on a calcareous plate which it secretes onto the rock.

On and under wave-washed rocks and other shells in the intertidal zone; it grows in shape to conform to its position. Florida to West Indies; B.C. to Peru in the west.

Some northwestern forms resemble limpets and have smooth concentric ridges rather than laminations; but they still have a spire, unlike true limpets. Bearded Hoof Shell, from the intertidal zone of Baja Calif., has a shaggy, brownish periostracum arranged in concentric rows.

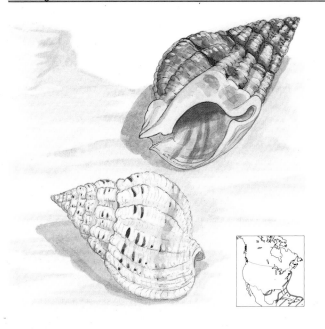

Inner wall of aperture shiny and greatly thickened. Axial ribs run from spire to aperture, crossed by spiral cords. Gray or white in color, often banded or spotted with dull brown.

A small heavy shell with a high conical pointed spire. Aperture oval with a notch at the top and a short siphonal canal at the base.

Near low tide levels on sand and mud flats; a scavenger. Cape Cod, Massachusetts to Florida, Texas, the Gulf states and the West Indies.

Dogwhelks occur on both coasts. Western Lean Nassa (found from Alaska to Baja Calif.) is yellow brown with spiral white bands. The orange brown Giant Western Nassa grows up to 2in high. Variable Nassa, from shallow waters off N. Carolina southwards, is white with yellow bands and strong axial ribs.

19

½–¾in high

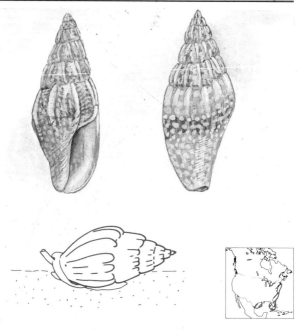

Yellow-brown shell with a pattern of white spots. Body whorl has between 7 and 21 heavy axial ribs, the northern shells having the highest number of ribs.

A thick, spindle-shaped shell with a high pointed spire. Aperture about half the length of the shell, pointed at the upper end, and with a short, broad siphonal canal.

Low tide level and shallow water amongst eelgrasses, where it feeds on bivalves and crustaceans. Massachusetts Bay to Florida and Texas.

Many other Dove Shells live off the southeast coast or in the Caribbean; many are very small and grow to ¼in high at most. Well-ribbed Dove Shell lives in similar situations to the Greedy Dove Shell; it is yellow or brown, sometimes with white spots, and has many ribs on all whorls.

This shell has keeled whorls. It is covered with a thick, brown periostracum which develops hairy bristles, especially on the three most prominent keels.

A rather fragile, white shell (beneath the periostracum) with a high, often eroded, spire. There are many spiral threads between the keels. Aperture large, pointed at the lower end. Umbilicus a small slit bordered by a large spiral cord.

On rocks or shells from just below low tide level to deep water; often cast up onto beaches. From the Arctic Ocean south to Maine in the Atlantic and to B.C. in the Pacific.

The larger Cancellate Hairy Shell grows up to 1in high. Its whorls have four or five strong spiral cords and it has a thick brown periostracum with bristles over the cords. It is found in shallow water from Alaska to Oregon.

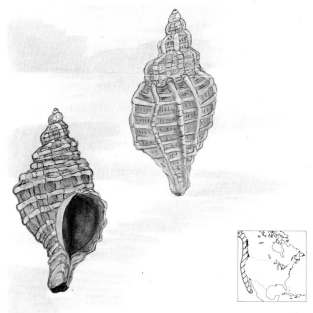

Strongly sculptured. Between 8 and 10 axial ribs crossed by alternating wide and narrow spiral cords produce a latticed effect.

A solid, spindle-shaped shell with a high spire, making up half the length of the shell. Siphonal canal is sealed over for part of its length. Light gray in color.

On rocks, in intertidal zone and shallow water; feeds on bivalves, drilling a hole into their shells. Alaska to Baja Calif.

Other dwarf tritons occur on the west coast, especially in Calif. Graceful Dwarf Triton lives on rock pilings. It has brown-spotted spiral cords. Japanese Rock Shell has strong spiral cords and ribs; introduced into B.C. and Washington. Adam's Dwarf Triton lives in Florida and West Indies.

There are flattened shoulders on the whorls and about 18 strong axial ribs, angled where they cross the shoulders. The whorls also bear numerous spiral threads.

A broadly spindle-shaped shell with a turreted spire and a large body whorl; the ribs on the body whorl fade towards the base. Aperture large and elongated, with a short siphonal canal. Creamy white to pale brown in color.

On sand and rubble, in water 30 to 400 feet deep. Arctic Ocean to Rhode Island in the east, Alaska to Puget Sound in the west. An important food source for haddock and other fishes.

There are many related shells on both coasts. Turriculate Lora has only 12–14 ribs and distinct spiral lines; it lives in deep water off both northern coasts. Incised Northern Lora is one of the most common off the northeast coast. It is whitish in color and only ¼in high, with shouldered whorls.

Coffee-colored or pinkish brown with three pairs of dark brown spots on the back. Many whitish ribs run from each side of the aperture, around the shell, to meet in the center of the back.

A dome-shaped shell, like a cowrie, apparently with no spire because the spire is inside the large body whorl. Aperture long and narrow, in central position beneath the shell. In life, most of the shell is covered by the mantle.

Associated with compound sea-squirts, in intertidal levels and shallow water down to 150 feet, in rocky areas. N. Carolina to Florida, Bermuda and the West Indies.

Other trivias, which are found on both coasts, are smaller. Little White Trivias are washed onto beaches from N. Carolina southwards; they are only ¼in long. Four-spotted Trivias are often washed onto Florida and West Indian beaches. When fresh they are pink with up to four small reddish spots on the back.

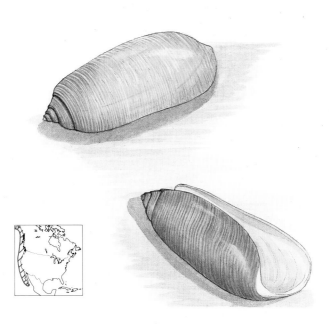

A yellow shell in which the body whorl has many fine spiral lines. There is a strong cord and a deep channeled suture at the junction of the body whorl and the spire.

A solid, cylindrical shell with a large body whorl and a low pointed, conical spire. Aperture long and narrow, widening at the base and with a thin outer margin.

On sand and mud from low tide level into shallow water and down to 150 feet. It burrows into the sand and feeds on other gastropods. Kodiak Island, Alaska to Baja Calif.

Channeled Barrel Bubble is smaller, cream-colored with darker staining. It lives in estuarine waters from Nova Scotia to the West Indies. Arctic Barrel Bubble is a tiny (only about ⅛in high) whitish shell which is found at low tide level from the Arctic Ocean to N. Carolina.

A greenish, globular shell, with a brownish periostracum. Aperture is approximately the same size as the body whorl. The outer margin of the aperture has a rounded wing at the top.

A thin, fragile, translucent shell. The large body whorl almost encloses the spire which appears only as a tiny apical hole. In life, the mantle partly covers the shell and the body cannot be entirely withdrawn into the shell.

In bays, in the intertidal zone and shallow water. Feeds on algae. Alaska to the Gulf of Calif.

Green Paper Bubble is found on open rocky western coasts. It is similar in color to Gould's Paper Bubble, but its aperture is larger than the body whorl. Other paper bubbles live on the east coast and in West Indies. Solitary Paper Bubble occurs on mud flats and sandy mud from Cape Cod to N. Carolina.

The shell has about 9–11 rounded ribs running axially from spire to aperture and many strong spiral cords. Aperture large, leading to a short, broad open siphonal canal.

A solid, oval shell. It has a high conical spire formed of convex, rounded whorls. Grayish or yellowish white in color, often with brown spiral bands. This species can be very destructive in oyster beds.

Usually in rocky areas or near oyster beds, from the intertidal zone into shallow water. Feeds on oysters. Nova Scotia to northeast Florida; Washington to central Calif.

Lurid Dwarf Triton is white or brown with many spiral threads; it grows about 1in high. It lives in intertidal and shallow waters from Alaska to Calif. **Carpenter's Dwarf Triton** is also found in the intertidal zone on the west coast; it has a closed siphonal canal.

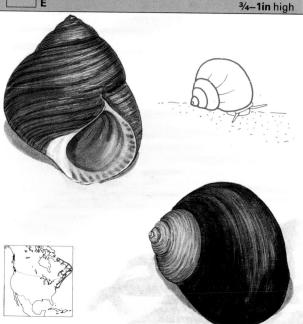

Olive-brown, often spirally banded with darker brown. Inside of aperture brown. Columella white; inside of outer lip white, often flecked with brown and with a brown edge.

A small solid shell, with smooth rounded whorls, a sharp apex and a round aperture. Edible and eaten in large quantities in Europe.

On rocky shores in the intertidal zone, amongst seaweeds and in tide pools. It feeds by grazing on seaweeds. From Labrador to Maryland.

Northern Yellow Periwinkle lives in the same habitats and range. It varies in color from yellow to orange or brown and has a low rounded spire. Rough Periwinkle occurs in the intertidal zone from the Arctic Ocean to New England; it is yellow or gray. Sitka Periwinkle lives on northwest coast.

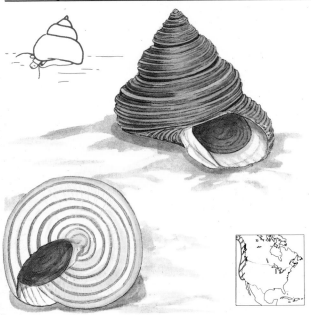

There are six to eight smooth, spiral, yellow-brown cords on each whorl, contrasting with a brown background. Worn patches appear blue.

A thick conical shell, with convex whorls and a pointed apex. The base of the shell is flat and the aperture is almost round. It has no umbilicus.

Intertidal in the northern part of its range, but in deeper water further south. Found under rocks or amongst seaweeds. Grazes on algae. Alaska to Central California.

Channeled Top Shell lives in the low tide levels and in shallow waters, from Alaska to Calif. It is conical, pale yellow and has many spiral cords. Jujube Top Shells may be washed up onto beaches of southeastern USA after storms; they have high, conical yellow-brown shells.

29

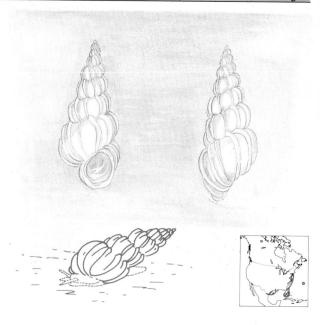

There are nine to ten strong, blade-like ribs on each whorl. They connect with ribs on the adjacent whorls at the suture lines.

A strong, tapering, white shell with a high spire. The eight whorls are smooth and separated at the sutures, connected only by the ribs. Aperture round, with a thickened outer lip.

In shallow water, in sand and often near sea anemones. Dead shells are often cast up onto beaches. From New York to Florida, Texas and Bermuda.

There are many similar wentletraps. Humphrey's Wentletrap, with a similar range, has nine to ten whorls with eight to nine ribs. Tinted Wentletrap is a similar species, found in intertidal levels and shallow water, from B.C. to Calif.; it has ten to twelve thick ribs on each whorl.

BORING TURRET SHELL ◆

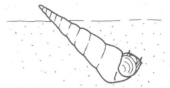

Yellowish or reddish brown shell with darker markings. There are numerous fine spiral threads on the whorls, some larger than others.

A slender, elongated shell with a pointed apex and 10–12 convex whorls. Aperture round with a thin outer lip and no siphonal canal.

In shallow, offshore waters where it burrows into sand; it is a filter feeder, filtering particles drawn into the shell with water. N. Carolina to Florida, Texas and West Indies.

There are many turret shells. Eastern Turret Shell has a large cord at the top and bottom of each whorl, with a concave area between; it occurs from N. Carolina to West Indies in offshore waters. Eroded Turret Shell is whitish, with spiral cords on convex whorls; it lives off north Atlantic and Pacific coasts.

This shell has many small, concentric, wavy cords giving it a striated appearance. Shelf on the inside is cup-like, attached by about one third of its circumference to the main shell.

A round, cup-shaped shell with the apex slightly off-center and twisted to one side. Outside yellow-gray; interior glossy, pale yellow or orange.

This animal feeds on particles which it filters from a current of water brought into the shell. It lives in shallow water on rocks and other shells, from Nova Scotia to Florida.

The whitish Circular Cup-and-saucer is found in shallow water from N. Carolina to Florida and West Indies; the shelf on the inside of the shell is attached by one side and slants towards the center. The Pacific Chinese Hat, from the west coast, has a sinuate edge to the cup inside, which arises from the apex.

PURPLE DWARF OLIVE

½–1¼in high

W

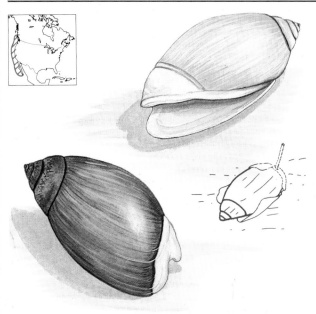

Light brown or whitish with violet markings around aperture and a dark purple-brown line beneath the channeled sutures. Columella folded at lower end with 2–4 spiral ridges.

A small, heavy, smooth shell with a large body whorl and a small conical spire. Inner wall of aperture white and thickened. Aperture narrow at the top and wide at the base; interior often purplish.

Sandy bays and beaches, burrowing into sand when tide is out, from low tide level to shallow water. Scavenger and predator, on bivalves and crustaceans. Vancouver Island to Baja Calif.

Most dwarf olives are smaller. The grayish-white Common Rice Olive and gray or brown Variable Dwarf Olive (which is often banded with white) both live in shallow water from N. Carolina to West Indies. Baetic Dwarf Olive (white or brown with a basal band of white) occurs from Alaska to Baja Calif.

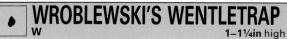

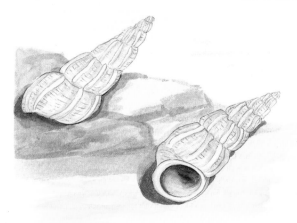

Six to eight low wide ribs run from the top of the spire to the base of the shell. Aperture round and bordered by a smooth, strong spiral cord.

A slender, tapering, solid shell with convex whorls, frequently beachworn. It is grayish-white in color and often stained with purple.

From rocks at low tide level to shallow water, and down to depths of 300ft. Feeds on sea anemones. Forester Island, Alaska to San Diego, Calif.

There are several similar wentletraps. The Scallop-edged Wentletrap is found on rocks at low tide level in Calif., associated with large sea anemones. Spongy Wentletrap lives in offshore waters from Oregon to Calif. Pumilio Wentletrap lives in shallow water from N. Carolina to Florida.

FINGERED LIMPET

1¼in long

W

Up to 25 coarse ribs extend from the apex to the margin of the shell, giving the margin a slightly wavy appearance. The apex is off-center, towards the front of the shell and hooked.

An asymmetrically cone-shaped shell. The outside is gray with irregular white stripes or spots; the inside is blue-white, with a central brown spot and a dark brown wavy border.

On rocks, close to the high tide mark of the intertidal zone, where it grazes on algae. Alaska to Baja Calif.

Rough Limpet has much heavier ridges and the apex of its shell is not hooked; it lives on high tide rocks from Oregon to Baja Calif. Shield Limpet has fine ribs radiating from the apex and no brown spot inside; it lives in the intertidal zone from Alaska to Baja Calif.

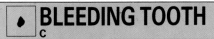

BLEEDING TOOTH
C

³/₄–1½in high

Light whitish yellow or gray with red and black zigzags. The white inner lip of the aperture has a blood red patch with two white teeth in it, one tooth larger than the other.

A thick, heavy, broadly cone-shaped shell with a low spire. Whorls are sculptured with spiral cords, strongest near the spire. These shells are sold in gift shops and are also used to make costume jewelry.

Found on rocky shores facing the open ocean, near low tide level. They graze on algae. Southeast Florida, Bermuda and the West Indies.

Four-toothed Nerite is found with Bleeding Tooth on exposed rocky shores. It has spirally arranged black and red zigzags and four white teeth on the white inner lip of the aperture. Zebra Nerite lives in tide pools on rocky shores above high tide level in southeast Florida, Bermuda and the West Indies.

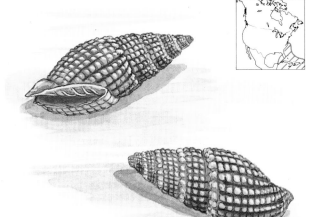

Neatly beaded; the effect is produced by about 17 narrow axial ribs crossed by 3–5 spiral cords. Orange-brown in color with paler, whitish beads.

A solid, spindle-shaped shell with a high spire, distinct suture lines between the whorls and slight shoulders on the whorls. Aperture narrow with four strong folds on the columella.

Under rocks at low tide and often washed up onto beaches. A carnivore, feeding on worms and other molluscs. N. Carolina to Florida, Bermuda and the West Indies.

Barbados Miter lives under rocks and reefs at low tide, from southeast Florida to West Indies; similar in shape and color to Beaded Miter but much smoother, with weak spiral threads. Beaded Florida Miter is darker brown and smaller, up to ⅜in; found from low tide to deep water from Florida to Bermuda.

A distinctively colored shell, pale whitish purple above and deep purple below.

A thin, fragile, smooth, rounded shell with a large body whorl and a low spire. It has a large aperture with a slightly wavy outer lip.

Floats on bubble rafts on the ocean, south from San Diego in the Pacific and from Nantucket in the Atlantic. Dead shells may be blown onto the southeast coast, especially in spring.

Other Purple Snails may be blown onto beaches. Pallid Purple Snail appears in Florida and Calif. in spring; it is rounded in shape and whitish purple in color. This is the commonest purple snail on the west coast. Elongate Purple Snail has an elongated, pointed aperture; it occurs on southern coasts.

DIRE WHELK

1–1½in high

W

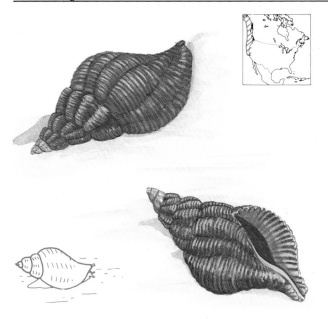

Dark gray or brown shell with a brown aperture. Low rounded axial ribs on the spire whorls are crossed by strong spiral cords; there are also strong spiral cords on the body whorl.

A solid, spindle-shaped shell, with a high pointed spire. Aperture large, with a thin but strong and finely serrated margin. Serrations continue as spiral ridges inside aperture. Short siphonal canal is slightly twisted to the left.

Rocky shores in the intertidal zone and in shallow water. Alaska to Monterey, Calif. A scavenger on molluscs, crabs, fishes and worms.

The Giant Western Nassa is pale orange-brown in color and has beaded spiral cords. It lives on sand and mud from low tide level to shallow water, from Vancouver Island to Baja Calif.

FLORIDA CERITH
E & C

1–1½in high

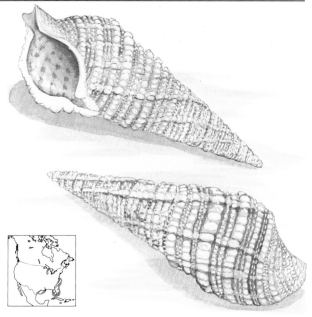

This whitish shell has red-brown spots. Each whorl has two or three white varices, with several rows of neat spiral beads and other finer beaded threads between them.

A slender, elongated shell with a pointed spire. Aperture small, an elongated oval with a short, broad siphonal canal.

Warm, shallow water on a sandy bottom or on rocks. Feeds on algae and plant remains. N. Carolina to Florida, Texas and the West Indies.

Dwarf Cerith grows up to half an inch high; it lives under rocks from the southern Florida coast to Texas and the West Indies. Stocky Cerith, from the same area, is larger but more stocky and oval in shape and has coarser beading. Pacific Fly-specked Cerith lives in shallow water in Baja Calif.

A purple-black shell, pearly white inside the aperture. The pearly white columella has two small knobs at the base and there is a white patch around the closed umbilicus.

A heavy, solid, top-shaped or dome-shaped shell with rounded whorls and slight wrinkles at the sutures. Aperture round.

Found amongst rocks in the intertidal zone. They graze on algae. From Vancouver to Baja Calif.

Other west coast Top Shells vary in color from yellow to gray, or may be mottled or banded. Dusky Top Shell is grayish with yellowish spots; it lives on intertidal rocks from Alaska to Calif. Brown Top Shell lives on rocks from Oregon to Calif. Others live on the southeastern coast and in the West Indies.

41

1–1¾in long

A distinctive, smooth, glossy shell, spindle-shaped with a transverse ridge across its back. Yellow to apricot in color with a wide white stripe along the back.

Aperture long and broad with inrolled margins. Mantle pale yellow with bright yellow, black-edged rings; it covers the shell in life and fragments may remain after death. Collected in large numbers and its numbers have seriously decreased.

Lives in shallow water on sea fans and sea whips, on which it feeds. N. Carolina to Florida, Bermuda and West Indies.

McGinty's Flamingo Tongue is similar, but the shell is more elongated and whitish tinged with pink. It is found in shallow water from N. Carolina to the West Indies.

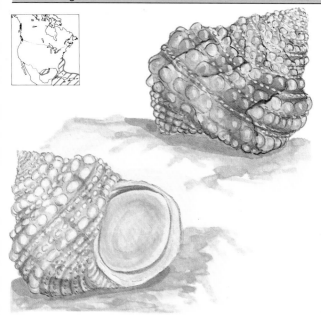

Brown or gray shell, sometimes greenish, decorated with lines of whitish beads or knobs and with vertical, white, flame-like markings.

A thick, top-shaped shell with a high spire, a round aperture and a closed umbilicus. The inside is pearly white.

Amongst and beneath rocks in shallow water, grazing on algae. N. Carolina to Florida and Texas, south to the West Indies.

The similar Wavy Turban is light brown; it lives at low tide level on the Calif. coast. Red Turban lives on rocks in shallow water, from B.C. to Baja Calif. Green Star Shell lives amongst rocks at low tide level in Florida and the West Indies; it is brown with white spots and broad axial ribs.

ATLANTIC SLIPPER SHELL
E, C & W

¾–2in long

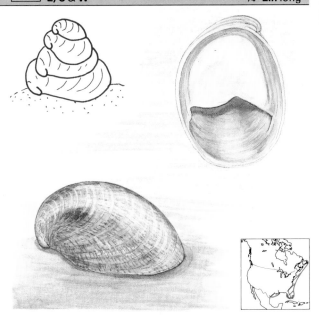

A boat-like shell, arched and with a low coiled apex at one end. The apex is bent to one side. There is a white, concave plate-like platform inside; this platform has a wavy edge.

A strong, low-arched, limpet-like shell, smooth or corrugated in texture and dirty white, purplish or brownish in color. Inside shiny white or brown. If present in large numbers these shells cause problems in oyster beds, by smothering oysters.

They live stacked up in piles, in shallow water on a muddy bottom. Dead shells are common on beaches. Southern Canada to Florida and Texas. Introduced to coast of Washington state.

The small Convex Slipper Shell lives on rocks in shallow water on the east coast and has been introduced to the west coast. It has a highly arched and dark brown shell. Spiny Slipper Shell has a spiny exterior, often covered with algae; it is found in shallow water from N. Carolina to Florida and Texas.

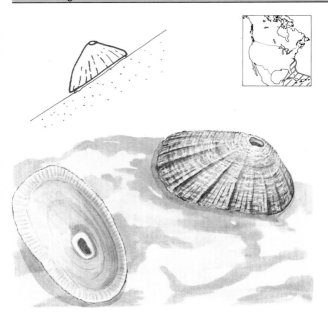

Keyhole-shaped hole at top of shell is positioned slightly in front of apex. Ridges radiate outwards from the apex of the shell, every fourth ridge larger than the others.

A solid, cone-shaped shell, with an oval base and no spire. Growth lines spiral around the shell.

On rocks, stones and seaweeds in the intertidal zone to water 100 feet deep. Feeds by grazing on algae. Maryland to Florida, Gulf of Mexico and West Indies.

Rough Keyhole Limpet is found from Alaska to Calif., on rocks or attached to kelp stalks, from low tide to shallow water. Two-spotted Keyhole Limpet occurs under stones and on kelp at low tide, from Alaska to Mexico; it has a large, oval-elongate hole at the apex. **Hooded Puncturella** has a hooked apex.

45

Atlantic form (illustrated) gray-white, mottled with red-brown. Pacific form greenish or brownish gray. Inside of shell bluish-white, with a central brown spot.

A smooth, low to medium height, cone-shaped shell, with no spire and a rounded oval base. The apex is more or less at the cone center.

Grazes on algae on intertidal rocks. Atlantic Plate Limpet occurs from Arctic Ocean to New York. Pacific Plate Limpet is common from Alaska to Oregon, rarer south to Baja Calif.

File Limpet is greenish-brown with fine ribs on a low cone; it lives on intertidal rocks from Puget Sound to Baja Calif. Mask Limpet is dark, speckled with white; it lives in intertidal rock crevices from Alaska to Calif. Fenestrate Limpet lives on smooth rocks on sandy beaches from Alaska to Baja Calif.

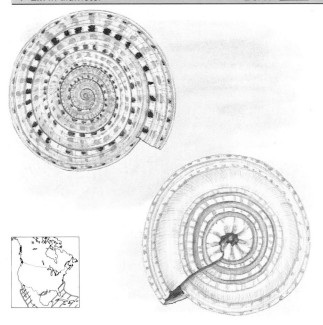

Distinctive, disk-like shell, heavily sculptured with spiral, beaded cords. Several of these cords are more prominent than the others.

A solid, flattened shell, yellow-white with red-brown spots especially noticeable just below the sutures. Umbilicus large and deep and bordered by a heavily beaded spiral cord.

In sand in shallow water, usually associated with sea pansies. From N. Carolina to Florida, Texas and the West Indies on the east coast; from Baja Calif. to Peru on the west coast.

Several other sundials occur in southern waters but are uncommon. Among them is the Bisulcate Sundial which is found in coastal waters from N. Carolina to the West Indies. It is creamy brown in color with a white central whorl, but only grows up to half an inch in diameter.

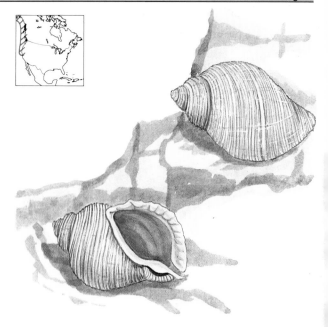

Up to 20 rounded spiral cords are present on the whorls, often one larger cord alternating with a smaller one. Several ridges run axially from the spire to the aperture.

An ovate, solid shell, with a large body whorl and a short, pointed spire. Whitish-gray or orange-brown in color. Aperture large, with a short siphonal canal.

Intertidal zone in rock crevices; feeds on barnacles and mussels. Alaska to Monterey, Calif.

There are other dogwinkles on the west coast. The Channeled Dogwinkle has a higher spire and about 15 flat-topped cords with deep channels between. The yellow and brown Emarginate Dogwinkle is more globular and has coarse, sculptured spiral ribs. Atlantic Dogwinkle is found from Labrador to New York.

Beaded, with numerous spiral cords crossed by weak axial ribs forming the beads. Creamy white to gray in color, with broken bands and lines of orange-brown.

A strong, heavy shell, broadly ovate in outline, with a large body whorl and pointed, conical spire. Aperture elongated with two spiral folds on the columella, the upper one crossed by one or two smaller folds.

In sand, amongst turtle grasses, from low tide line to shallow water. N. Carolina to Florida, Texas and the West Indies.

Other nutmegs are found on the southern coasts and in the Caribbean but none are very common. Rugose Nutmeg, from the West Indies, is dirty white with brown bands, it has shouldered whorls and a sculpture of strong axial ribs; it grows up to 1in long.

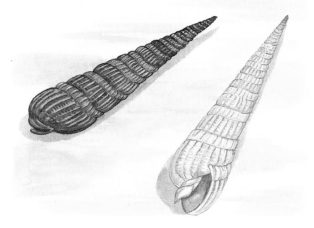

The shell is actually composed of about 15 whorls, but there is a wide spiral band beneath the suture, which gives the shell the appearance of having twice as many whorls.

A slender, elongated shell with a pointed apex. There are about 25 axial ribs on each whorl. Aperture small and siphonal canal is twisted to the left at the base of the columella. Usually pinkish gray but sometimes blue-gray or yellowish.

In sand, from low tide level to deep water. Maryland to Florida, Texas and the West Indies. Also in Calif., south from Los Angeles. A carnivore, feeding on worms.

Other augers live off southern coasts, many in the Gulf of Calif. Salle's Auger (from northwestern Florida to Mexico) is dark brown with small ribs extending half way down each whorl. Gray Atlantic Auger is similar but cream or light brown. San Pedro Auger lives in shallow water off coast of Baja Calif.

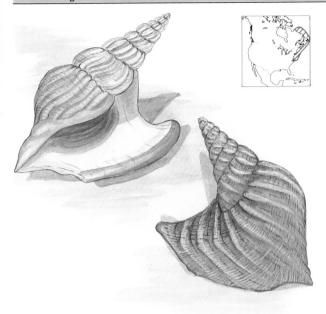

Outer lip of the aperture is expanded into a white winglike projection. The edge of this lip is thickened and colored.

An elongated shell, with a high pointed spire, yellow or light gray in color. The whorls are rounded, each with 15–25 curved axial ribs and many tiny spiral threads.

On a sandy or muddy bottom in water 30–180 feet deep, where it feeds on detritus and algae. Labrador to N. Carolina.

No similar species.

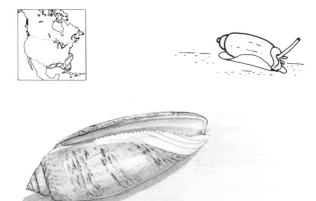

Light grayish-brown in color, with many fine purple-brown zigzag markings, especially on the body whorl.

A smooth, glossy, heavy shell with a large, cylindrical body whorl and a conical, pointed spire. Aperture long and narrow, with a white thickened inner wall; this wall broadens towards the lower end and has four low spiral ridges.

Beneath sand by day, crawling over the sand at night, in lower intertidal zone and shallow water. Mantle and foot cover the shell in life. N. Carolina to Texas and the Gulf states.

Netted Olive lives in sand in shallow water from southeastern Florida to the West Indies. It is smaller and rounder than the Lettered Olive, white and with deeply channeled suture lines on the spire. Veined Olive lives in the Gulf of Calif.; it has many brown zigzag markings on a yellow-gray shell.

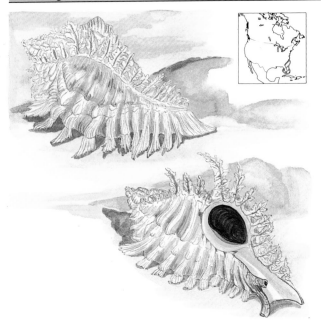

The three varices on each whorl bear long, scaly, hollow spines. There are also 8–10 leafy, scaly spines on the outer edge of the aperture and outer edge of the siphonal canal.

A broadly elongated shell with a large body whorl and a high conical spire, light brown or whitish in color. The spire bears an axial rib between each varix and fine spiral cords. Aperture small and round.

On sand, amongst rocks and rubble, or in muddy areas with mangroves; from the intertidal zone to shallow water. Feeds on bivalves. S. Carolina to southern Florida.

West Indian Lace Murex is larger and darker. Cabrit's Murex grows up to 2½in high and has a long slender siphonal canal with many spines. Giant Eastern Murex grows 5–7in high; it is light gray with strong straight spines on canal and on varices. Both occur from the Carolinas to the West Indies.

53

SHARK EYE

E & C

1–2½in high; nearly **3in** in diameter

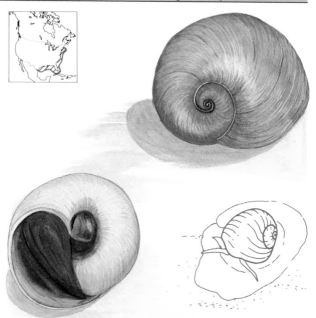

The early, central whorls are darker than the outer whorls, giving the appearance of an eye to the shell. Umbilicus deep but covered by a brown button-like callus.

A rounded, smooth, glossy shell with 4 or 5 whorls, a convex base and a low spire; it is usually much wider than high. Gray or brown in color, with a white base and a brown interior. The aperture is half-moon shaped.

Sandy areas, from intertidal zone to shallow water. It burrows through the sand, searching for clams on which it feeds. Cape Ann, Massachusetts to Florida and Gulf States.

Milk Moon Shell, with same range as Shark Eye, is white. Colorful Atlantic Natica is pale yellow, streaked with red; found in shallow water from N. Carolina southwards. Arctic Natica has a brown periostracum over a white shell; found in deep water from Arctic Ocean to N. Carolina and Calif.

ATLANTIC CARRIER SHELL

1–3in wide without attached fragments

E & C

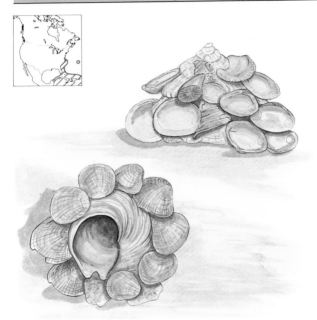

This shell has many fragments of shells, stones or coral attached to its upper surface, in a spiral which follows the whorl formation, smallest fragments in the center.

A top-shaped shell, quite heavy and solid, with no umbilicus. It is yellow-brown in color beneath the fragments. From above it looks like a moving pile of debris when alive. Usually an individual attaches only one kind of debris to itself.

On sandy bottoms amongst rubble in shallow water, where it feeds on detritus. N. Carolina to Bermuda and the West Indies.

Caribbean Carrier Shell has only a few shell fragments attached. It is white and fragile and has a large, round umbilicus. It is found from S. Carolina to the West Indies, in relatively deep water.

55

Pale yellow with three or more spiral rows of squarish red-brown spots. Usually there are about 20 spiral grooves on the large body whorl.

A thick, ovate shell with a large body whorl and a low, pointed spire. The outer lip of the large aperture is thickened and toothed; the lower part of the inner lip is roughened, with raised spots.

Creeps about on sand in shallow water; feeds on sea urchins. N. Carolina to Texas and West Indies; also from the Gulf of Calif. to Ecuador. May be washed up onto beaches after storms.

A smooth form of this shell, from the West Indies, lacks the spiral grooves. The similar Royal Bonnet occurs in deep water from southeastern Florida to Texas and the West Indies; it is about 2in high, with a smooth inner lip to the aperture and has a higher spire than the Scotch Bonnet.

FLORIDA ROCK SHELL

E & C

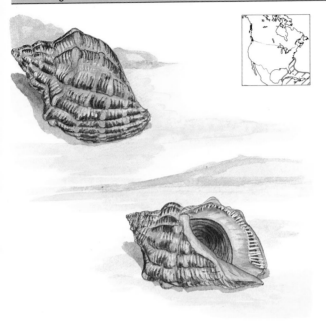

Gray or yellow with many brown spots and bars. Aperture ovate, with a short siphonal canal, salmon pink inside. Outer lip has many white spiral ridges on a brown background.

A solid shell with a large body whorl and a pointed conical spire. Usually many spiral cords on the whorls and often two rows of knobs on the body whorl. Columella almost straight, creamy yellow or orange. Can damage oysters and clams.

Intertidal zone to below low tide level; feeds on bivalves, including oysters and clams, and barnacles. N. Carolina to Florida, Bermuda, Gulf of Mexico and West Indies.

Hay's Rock Shell, from northwest Florida and Texas, is larger (up to 4½in high), a more rugged shell. Rustic Rock Shell (Florida southwards) is gray with a white aperture and brown outer lip. The gray and brown Deltoid Rock Shell has two rows of large knobs; found from Florida to West Indies in surf.

White with a spiral pattern of rows of orange-brown spots or squares. Covered with a thin, light brown periostracum when fresh. Aperture long and narrow with a white interior.

A big cone-shaped shell. It has a large body whorl and a flat top with a small conical spire. It is smooth in texture except for a series of spiral ridges near the base of the shell. This animal, like the other cones, has a sting like a bee.

In sand, in shallow water. A carnivore, capturing its prey with poisonous harpoon-like teeth (the sting) and feeding on worms and gastropods. Florida and the Gulf states to Mexico.

The mottled brown **Mouse Cone** grows up to 1½in high; it has knobs on the shoulder of the body whorl. The smaller, orange-spotted Jasper Cone has spiral ridges on spire and body. Both come from Florida, Bermuda and the West Indies. The Calif. Cone is grayish white with a thick brown periostracum.

Fresh shells have a brown periostracum covered with rows of hairs. Aperture brown, large with a narrow, straight canal; inner lip has many long white teeth on a brown background.

An elongated, high-spired shell, with spiral sculpturing. There are thick varices on each whorl, two thirds of a whorl apart. Gray-brown or brown in color, beneath the periostracum.

Intertidal pools and shallow water, beneath rocks or buried in sand. It feeds on bivalves. Found on both coasts; from S. Carolina to Texas, Bermuda and the West Indies; Gulf of Calif.

There are many other tritons, especially in the Caribbean, where Angular and Goldmouth Tritons are found. Trumpet Triton grows up to 13in high; it is common in the West Indies in shallow water near reefs. Oregon Triton is a west coast species which grows 5in high; it has a bristly brown periostracum.

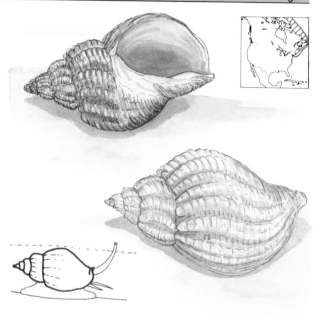

The shell has 9–18 curved axial ribs on the spire whorls, extending half way down the body whorl. It also has many spiral cords.

A heavy solid shell with a conical pointed spire and convex whorls. Yellow-gray in color. Aperture, columella and inner and outer lips of aperture white. Aperture large and ovate with a short siphonal canal. Edible and eaten in Europe.

From just offshore to shallow water, on sand or mud. A scavenger, feeding on dead and dying animals. Arctic Ocean to New Jersey.

Silky Whelk occurs in offshore waters on both northern coasts, into the Arctic Ocean. It is light brown, up to 2½in long, with numerous intertwining axial ribs and tiny spiral beaded threads. Glacial Whelk has a similar distribution. It is purple-brown with a keel on the top and bottom of each whorl.

Shoulder of shell bears a row of hollow triangular spines which usually point upwards. Other spines may be present on the spire and blunter spines may occur on the body whorl.

A large shell with an inflated body whorl and a broad, conical spire. Cream-colored with variable spiral bands of brown or black. Aperture large with a very broad siphonal canal; interior banded in brown and cream.

On mud and sand in lagoons and bays, often amongst mangroves; from intertidal level into shallow water. Scavenger, feeding on living and dead animals. Florida, Gulf States and Mexico.

West Indian Crown Conch is larger, with a wide aperture and with a thick white margin around the aperture. Pacific Crown Conch is purplish to dark brown with white bands; it occurs on intertidal mud flats in the Gulf of Calif.

APPLE MUREX
E & C

2—4in high

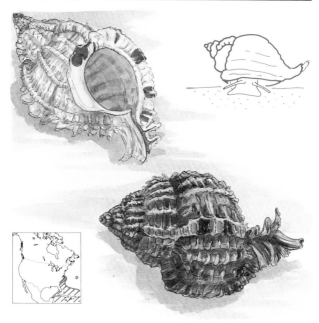

This murex has no long spines. The aperture is shiny, with a dark brown spot on the broad upper edge of the inner wall and three or four brown spots on the thickened, wavy outer wall.

A rough, heavy, yellow brown to dark brown shell with a broad conical spire. It has a sculptured appearance, with many knobs and cords and three varices on each whorl. The siphonal canal is short and broad and has an upturned end.

Intertidal areas and shallow water, on sand and amongst rocks. It feeds on oysters, boring a hole into the shell. N. Carolina to Florida, West Indies and Bermuda.

There are many other murexes off the southeastern coast, especially in the Caribbean, and off Calif. The **Pitted Murex** is small and rough, with fluted varices on the whorls. Bent-beak Murex is orange or pink with spineless varices. Many murexes, like the **Lace Murex** have longer spines.

FLORIDA FIGHTING CONCH

3–4in high

E & C

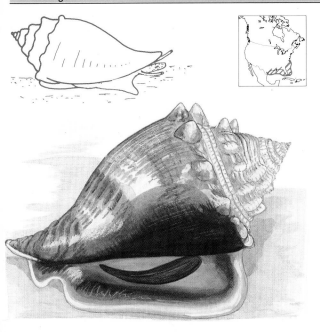

Outer lip of aperture forms a winglike projection with a V-shaped notch near the siphonal canal. Short spines may or may not be present on the shoulder of the last whorl.

A large heavy shell with a short conical spire and a very large body whorl. Dark reddish brown, often with paler spots or zigzag stripes on the shiny inner lip of the aperture. Spire whorls bear axial ribs and spiral cords.

In sand in shallow warm water, usually amongst marine grasses. N. Carolina to Florida (especially on the west coast) and Texas. Claw-like operculum used in movement and defence.

Conchs live on both southern Atlantic and Pacific coasts. West Indian Fighting Conch has spines on the last two whorls. Pink Conch grows up to 12in high; it is found from southeast Florida to West Indies. Milk Conch, from Florida, Bermuda and West Indies, is 4–7in long and has no knobs on the spire.

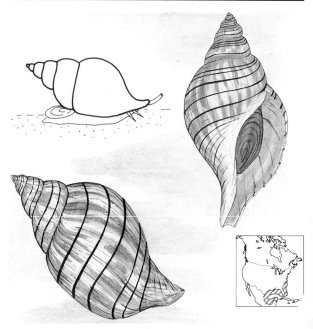

A creamy or gray shell with mauve or yellow vertical markings. It has 7–11 unbroken, purple-brown spiral lines on the body whorl and similar lines on the spire whorls.

A smooth spindle-shaped shell with a large body whorl and a high pointed spire. Aperture long and oval with a long slender, open siphonal canal.

On sand and mud flats from the intertidal zone to shallow water. Carnivorous, feeding on gastropods and bivalves. N. Carolina to Florida, Gulf states, Yucatan and Mexico.

The similar True Tulip grows up to 8in high. It has many broken lines and blotches instead of unbroken spiral lines. It is found on intertidal sand and mud and in shallow water from N. Carolina to Texas and the West Indies. Florida Horse Conch grows up to 19in high, the largest gastropod in N. America.

2½–5in high

W

The largest Moon Shell, it has slight shoulders on the whorls below the sutures. Umbilicus deep but partly covered by a small, brown-stained callus extending from the columella.

A large, globular shell with 4 or 5 whorls, a large body whorl and a low spire. It is yellow-white in color with a thin brown periostracum that rubs off easily. Aperture is half-moon shaped.

Sandy areas, from the intertidal zone into water 180ft deep. It burrows through the sand, searching for clams on which it feeds. Vancouver Island south to Baja Calif.

Common Northern Moon Shell lives in the intertidal zone from the Gulf of St Lawrence to N. Carolina. It has no callus over the umbilicus. Pale Northern Moon Shell, white with a pale yellow periostracum, lives in offshore waters on both coasts, from the Arctic Ocean to N. Carolina and Calif.

COUE'S SPINDLE SHELL

C

3–5in

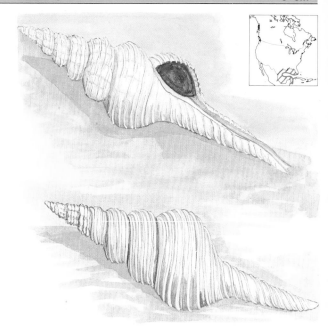

A graceful white shell with a high pointed spire, a small ovate aperture and a very elongated siphonal canal. The canal has a narrow channel.

This is a heavy spindle-shaped shell. It has numerous strong spiral threads, and broad axial ribs on the uppermost spire whorls. It is covered by a thin, straw-yellow periostracum.

Found on sand in offshore waters from 30 to 100 feet deep, in the Gulf of Mexico. Commonly dredged up by shrimp fishermen.

Turnip Spindle Shell, from the Gulf of Mexico, has a conical spire and a rounder, broader body whorl. It is white, tinged with orange. White Giant Turrid and Delicate Giant Turrid have strong double spiral cords on the spire whorls and fine axial ribs; both come from the southeast coast and the Caribbean.

66

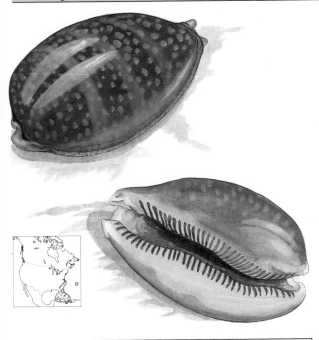

A large, glossy, colorful shell, brownish with many small whitish spots on the back. Aperture long and narrow with toothed lips.

The largest cowry in American waters. Its domed shape comes from enclosure of the spire in the large body whorl. Mantle extends over most of the shell in life. A valued collector's item, its numbers are threatened by overcollecting.

From low tide level to depths of 50 feet or more. It hides by day beneath rocks and reefs and emerges by night to feed on detritus and algae. N. Carolina to Florida, Bermuda and Cuba.

The similar Measled Cowry is smaller, with fewer large spots and the spots on its sides have brown centers. **Gray Cowries** and Yellow Cowries are smaller, up to 1½in long; they are found from N. Carolina to West Indies. Chestnut Cowry, from Calif., grows up to 2in long and is brown with white spots.

Each spire whorl has two raised cords, often strongly developed, which may be darker in color than the rest of the shell. There are up to eight similar cords on the body whorl.

A solid heavy shell with a large body whorl and a turret-like spire. Whitish-brown in color with a white aperture. The siphonal canal is short, open and twisted backwards.

From low tide level into shallow water in the north, in deeper water in the south, on sand or mud. A scavenger. Arctic Ocean to central Calif.

There are many other less common neptunes living in offshore waters, off both northern coasts. New England Neptune is gray white, with 7–10 strong red-brown cords on the body whorl and two similar cords on each spire whorl. It lives in deep water from the Grand Banks to N. Carolina.

BLACK ABALONE
W

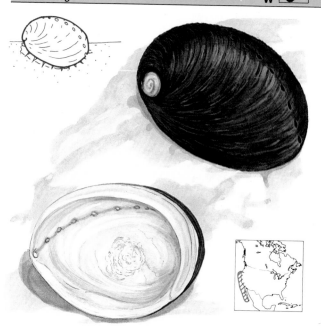

From five to eight holes present on outside margin, openings flush with the surface. Outside of shell bluish or greenish black, inside pearly white with pink or green reflections.

A thick, ear-shaped shell with a low, flattened spire towards one end. Outside of shell is smooth, with indistinct growth lines. Edible but not of commercial value, because of its small size and dark flesh.

Found clinging to rocks where it feeds by grazing on algae, from the intertidal zone into shallow water. Coos Bay, Oregon to Baja Calif.

Most other abalones are larger, rougher shells which live in deeper water. **Red Abalones** (found from Oregon to Calif.) are prized for their flesh and their color. The Californian Pink Abalones are also considered a delicacy. Japanese Abalones are gray-brown and most widely distributed, from Alaska to Calif.

A distinctive, cream-colored shell with spiral rows of squarish red-brown spots.

A smooth, solid, spindle-shaped shell with a very large body whorl. It has a small pointed spire with distinct sutures. The large aperture is elongated and has a short siphonal canal. A collector's shell.

In sand, in water 40 to 250 feet deep. N. Carolina to Florida, Texas and Mexico. Specimens are brought ashore by fishermen and others are washed onto beaches in small numbers.

Dohrn's Volute is more slender, 3–4in high, and has fine, incised spiral lines. It is found off the south Florida coast. Dubious Volute, found in waters off southern Florida and in the Gulf of Mexico, is also slender, and lighter than the other two; it has only 5–8 rows of spots.

Spire whorls terraced, with strongly ridged shoulders and deep channels at the sutures. In life these shells have a gray, felt-like periostracum.

A large, creamy-gray, pear-shaped shell with a rounded body whorl that narrows into a long, slightly curved siphonal canal. Aperture wide, yellow-brown inside. Edible and used as a food during the early part of the century.

On sand and mud, from intertidal zone to below low tide level. Scavenger and predator on molluscs, including oysters. Cape Cod to northern Florida; introduced into San Francisco Bay.

The Lightning Whelk, brown with axial red-brown markings, is coiled sinistrally and has a row of knobs on the shoulder of the body whorl; occurs from N. Carolina to Texas. The whitish Knobbed Whelk occurs from Cape Cod to Cape Canaveral; it has knobs on the body whorl shoulder and an orange aperture.

A massive shell, with a large body whorl and a low spire; pale yellow-white in color. There is a row of knobs on the shoulder of the body whorl and two more rows of smaller knobs below.

Inner lip of aperture triangular, broad and shield-like with long whitish teeth on a brown background; outer lip also broad and has 10–12 teeth with brown spots between. Shells cut and made into cameos or used as souvenirs; meat used in chowders.

It creeps about on sand in shallow water and feeds on sea urchins. N. Carolina to Bermuda and the larger islands of the West Indies.

King Helmet is common in sandy shallow waters of the West Indies but rarer off coast of southeast USA. It grows up to 9in high and is patterned with dark brown zigzags. The Flame Helmet, from the Caribbean, grows up to 6in high and is brown with darker markings.

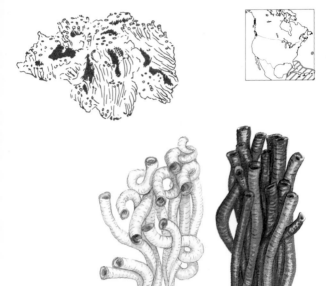

Forms tight colonies of upright, orange or brown tubes. The surface of the shell is coarsely ridged and wrinkled with growth lines. Individual tubes less than ¹⁄₁₆in across.

Variable in form, depending on habitat. In quiet waters off the Florida coast, it forms large dark reefs. In the intertidal zone the colonies grow flat to the surface of the rocks. West Indian forms are lighter in color and looser in form.

Attached to rocks in intertidal and shallow waters, from Florida to the West Indies and Bermuda. These are filter feeders, feeding on minute particles in water drawn into the shell.

Irregular Worm Shell has coiled shells, twisted to form large colonies on rocks in shallow water, from Florida to West Indies. Whitish worm-like shells of Compact Worm Shell occur in offshore waters, from Washington to Calif., on shells and rocks; the loosely coiled mass measures about an inch across.

OTHER SMALL GASTROPODS

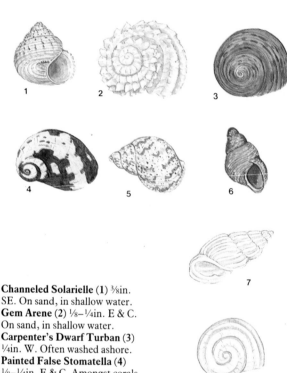

Channeled Solarielle (1) ⅜in. SE. On sand, in shallow water. **Gem Arene** (2) ⅛–¼in. E & C. On sand, in shallow water. **Carpenter's Dwarf Turban** (3) ¼in. W. Often washed ashore. **Painted False Stomatella** (4) ⅛–¼in. E & C. Amongst corals in shallow water. **Spotted Pheasant Shell** (5) ¼in. SE & C. On turtle grass in shallow water. **Compact Alvania** (6) ⅛in. W. Among seaweeds, low tide to deep water. **Catesby's Risso** (7) ⅛in. E & C. In shallow bays & lagoons. **Suppressed Vitrinella** (8) ¹⁄₁₆in wide. SE. Under rocks in shallow water. **Beautiful Caecum** (9) ¹⁄₁₆in. E & C. In eelgrass, in bays and lagoons.

OTHER SMALL GASTROPODS

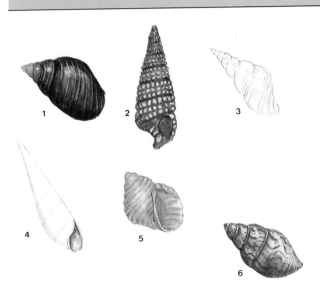

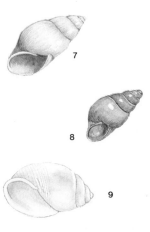

Atlantic Planaxis (**1**) ¼in. SE &
C. In shelter, in intertidal zone.
Black-lined Trifora (**2**) ⅛–¼in.
E & C. Beneath seaweeds at low
tide. **Varicose Alaba** (**3**) ¼–⅜in.
SE & C. In sand & weeds
in shallow water. **Carpenter's
Melanella** (**4**) ¼–⅜in. W. On
sand in shallow water.
Fenestrate Fossarus (**5**) ¼in.
W. In mussel beds. **Lunar Dove
Shell** (**6**) ¼in. E & C. Among
seaweeds, at low tide. **Fine-
sculptured Odostome** (**7**) ⅛–¼in.
W. On oysters & abalones in
shallow water. **Brown Sayella**
(**8**) ¼in. E. In mud, amongst
eelgrass in shallow water.
Adam's Baby Bubble (**9**) ⅛–¼in.
E & C. Amongst seaweeds in
shallow water.

OTHER GASTROPODS

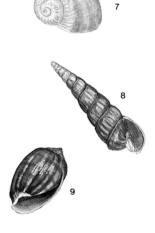

Striated Margarite (1) ½in. E. On seaweeds, intertidal to deep water. **Virgin Nerite** (2) ½in. SE & C. Intertidal flats & mangrove roots. **Northern Yellow Periwinkle** (3) ⅓–½in. NE. Amongst seaweeds on intertidal rocks. **Common Prickly Winkle** (4) ½–¾in. SE & C. On rocks near high tide. **Giant Pacific Coast Bittium** (5) ½–¾in. W. Among rocks in intertidal & shallow water. **Common West Indian Simnia** (6) ½in. E & C. On sea whips in shallow water. **Livid Natica** (7) ¼–¾in. SE & C. Intertidal sand flats. **Adam's Pyram** (8) ½–¾in. SW. Sand & mud flats at low tide. **Calif. Melampus** (9) ½in. SW. Mud flats near high tide.

OTHER GASTROPODS

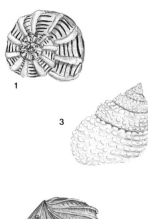

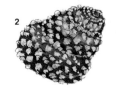

Atlantic Modulus (1) ½–¾in. E & C. Amongst grasses in warm shallow water. **False Prickly Winkle (2)** ½–1in. SE & C. Above high tide line. **Beaded Periwinkle (3)** 1in. SE & C. Above high tide line. **Hooded Puncturella (4)** ¾–1in. W. Among rocks in shallow water. **False Limpet (5)** ½–1in. E & C. On rocks near high tide. **Atlantic Gray Cowrie (6)** ¾–1½in. E & C. On reefs in shallow water. **Livid Macron (7)** 1in. SW. Low tide rocks. **Pitted Murex (8)** 1in. E & C. Intertidal & shallow water.

OTHER GASTROPODS

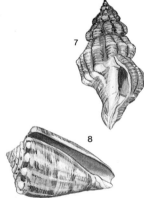

Long-spined Star Shell (**1**) 2–2½in wide. SE & C. Shallow water, in turtle grass. **Calif. Horn Shell** (**2**) 1–1½in. SW. Intertidal mud flats. **Atlantic Distorsio** (**3**) 1–3½in. E & C. On sand in shallow water. **Thorn Drupe** (**4**) 1–1½in. W. Intertidal rocks. **Festive Murex** (**5**) 1½–2in. SW. Mud flats, pilings & rocks in shallow water. **Short Coral Shell** (**6**) ¾–2in. SE & C. Base of corals in shallow water. **Chestnut Latirus** (**7**) 1–2in. SE & C. Under intertidal rocks. **Mouse Cone** (**8**) 1–1½in. SE & C. Around rocks in shallow water.

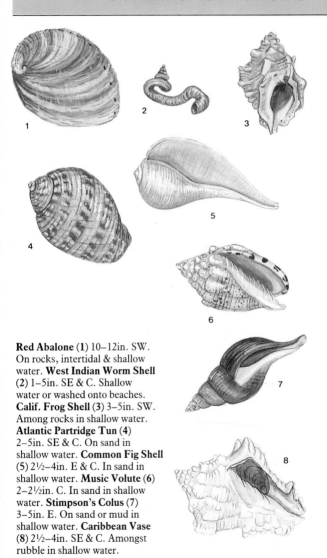

Red Abalone (1) 10–12in. SW. On rocks, intertidal & shallow water. **West Indian Worm Shell (2)** 1–5in. SE & C. Shallow water or washed onto beaches. **Calif. Frog Shell (3)** 3–5in. SW. Among rocks in shallow water. **Atlantic Partridge Tun (4)** 2–5in. SE & C. On sand in shallow water. **Common Fig Shell (5)** 2½–4in. E & C. In sand in shallow water. **Music Volute (6)** 2–2½in. C. In sand in shallow water. **Stimpson's Colus (7)** 3–5in. E. On sand or mud in shallow water. **Caribbean Vase (8)** 2½–4in. SE & C. Amongst rubble in shallow water.

Each valve has about 12 strong, knobbly radial ribs. The exterior is yellow-brown mottled with darker brown spots. Interior purplish.

Small and thick-shelled, somewhat inflated. More or less diamond-shaped, with an elongated, rounded hind end. The small beaks are near the front end.

Attached to the undersides of stones and rocks, and to pilings, from low tide level to water 300 feet deep. B.C. to northern Baja Calif.

Broad-ribbed Cardita comes from Florida and the Gulf coast; it is similar but much larger, 1–1½in long, and has a pale grayish exterior with strong radial ribs and red-brown spots. It lives in sand and mud in shallow water and is used in shell craft. Other carditas are more rounded in outline.

Very fragile, almost translucent shell with a gaping hind end. It is whitish in color with a thin, brown periostracum and often has sand grains attached to it.

Elongated, with the front end inflated and the hind end compressed and tapering; it is often truncated at the hind end. The hinge is weak and without teeth, but has prominent beaks.

Nestles into sand, from low tide level into deep water. From Nova Scotia to S. Carolina.

Sandy Lyonsia occurs in shallow water on northern coasts. It is flattened, has a heavy yellow-green periostracum and attaches sand grains to itself. Calif. Lyonsia is found in mud in shallow water, from Alaska to Baja Calif.; it is similar to Glassy Lyonsia, about 1in long and almost transparent.

This shell has up to 10 to 15 prominent, concentric, brown-stained growth lines. It is pinkish-white with a thin yellowish periostracum, and a whitish interior flushed with orange pink.

A broadly ovate, quite solid shell with pointed beaks and a blunt hind end.

In sand, from the low tide level into deep water. Aleutian Islands to San Pedro, Calif.

Faust Tellin and Smooth Tellin, both from West Indies, are large (2–4in) white shells. Many tellins are more elongated, like **Alternate Tellin**. Carpenter's Tellin and Modest Tellin, both west coast species, are quite elongated, the first creamy white tinged with pink, and the latter iridescent white.

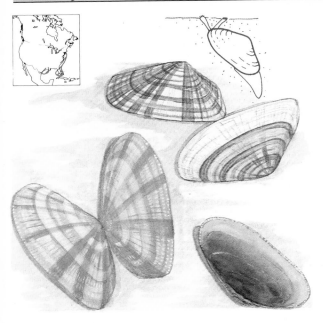

Whitish with rays of pink, purple, orange, yellow, brown or blue and often banded as well as rayed with color. Brightly colored inside with similar colors.

A wedge-shaped shell with a short hind end and an elongated front end. The valves often remain attached together by a strong ligament after death. Makes very good chowder.

Just below the surface of sand from mid to low tide level, moving with the tide and burrowing quickly into the sand when uncovered. New York to Florida and Texas.

Gould's Donax or Bean Clam lives in sandy Calif. beaches; it is cream, banded with purple-brown, and has a brown interior. Small False Donax lives in southern sandy beaches and West Indies; it has an oval shell. Sunrise Tellin (S. Carolina to West Indies) has rays of pink or yellow and a yellow interior.

Chalk-white, but covered with a smooth, shining, yellow-brown periostracum which is often worn away over the beaks.

A thin, inflated shell, broadly oval in shape. It has fine concentric growth lines on the exterior and a whitish interior. The beaks are nearly central and rounded teeth form the hinge.

Attached to wharf pilings, in mussel beds and amongst jewel boxes, from the intertidal zone to shallow water. Alaska to Calif.

North Atlantic Kellia lives in shallow water on both coasts, in rock crevices and attached to shells; it grows up to ½in long, a fat white shell with a yellow periostracum. Other related species live on both coasts; they are generally smaller and less common.

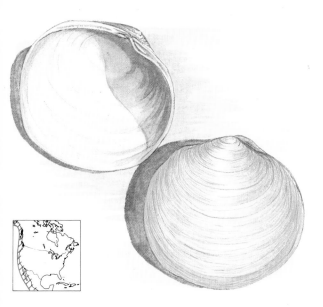

Round and almost globular in outline, with coarse concentric growth lines. White with a thin yellow-brown periostracum and a white interior.

The beaks of this shell are small, more or less central and point forwards. There are two large teeth in each hinge below the beaks; one of the two teeth is split in each valve.

Under rocks and in empty shells where it builds a nest of pieces of periostracum or detritus, with long tubes for the siphons. Alaska to the Gulf of Calif.

Other diplodons are found on both coasts. Common Atlantic Diplodon grows up to ¾in long and lives in sand from N. Carolina to Florida and the West Indies. It is similar in appearance to the Pacific Orb Diplodon but the periostracum is usually rubbed away.

Chalky white in color, sometimes with brown markings. The exterior has many flat radial ribs with narrow channels between them.

A solid, nearly round shell, slightly inflated. It has small prominent beaks and a curved hinge line with many small teeth. The shell has a heavy periostracum in life but this may be worn away so that it only remains at the margins.

Burrows in sand in shallow to deep water from the Aleutian Islands to Baja Calif. Single valves are often washed onto beaches.

Atlantic Bittersweet grows up to 2in long; it is creamy white with brown blotches, relatively smooth except for fine radial and concentric lines. Comb Bittersweet is grayish white with raised, brown radial ribs; it grows ½–1in long. Both live in shallow water from N. Carolina to the West Indies.

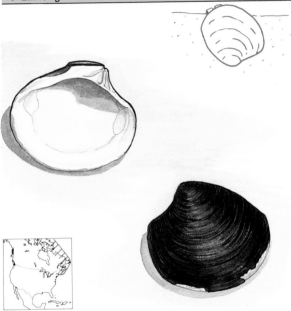

This shell is covered with a thick brown periostracum which flakes at the margins. There are strong concentric ridges near the beaks but these fade out towards the margins.

Thick-shelled, white beneath the periostracum and with a white interior. It is broadly oval in outline, with small central beaks which point forwards.

On a sandy or muddy bottom, with stones and gravel. From shallow water 30 feet deep into deep water. Arctic Ocean to Massachusetts on the east coast and to Alaska in the west.

There are other astartes in deep northern waters. Lentil Astarte occurs from the Arctic Ocean to Florida. Waved Astarte occurs from Labrador to New Jersey. Both species have strong concentric ridges. Smooth and Elliptical Astartes live in northeastern waters, Alaskan Astarte in northwestern waters.

87

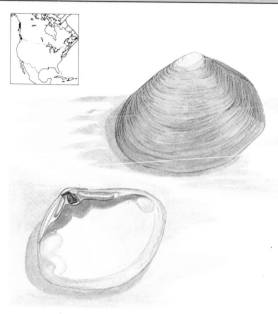

Wedge-shaped shell, with a large brown ligament in a spoon-shaped pit beneath each beak. On each side of the pit there are long teeth which have comb-like serrations.

A white shell with thin yellowish periostracum. Thick-shelled, somewhat flattened from side to side, smooth but with fine growth lines. The beaks are about a third of the way along the shell, from the front end. Interior white with brown margins.

Burrows into sand from intertidal zone to water 40 feet deep. Arctic Ocean to Chesapeake Bay.

The very similar Turton's Wedge Clam is found in the Gulf of St Lawrence. The **Atlantic Surf Clam** is superficially similar but much bigger.

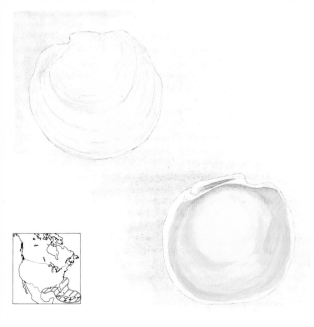

Interior of shell tinged with yellow near the margins, white in the center. Exterior smooth, dull white with concentric growth lines.

An almost round, inflated shell with central beaks. The beaks point forwards and there is a distinct heart-shaped depression in front of the beaks, half in each valve. Used in shell craft.

In sand, from shallow water to water 300 feet deep. Single valves are often found on sandy beaches. N. Carolina to Florida, the Gulf states and the West Indies.

There are many small lucines on all coasts, white or yellow in color and most 1in or less in length. Cross-hatched Lucine, from the southeast coast and the Caribbean, is white with a criss-cross pattern of curving lines. Fine-lined Lucine, from offshore waters on the west coast, is chalky white.

Shiny, light green to tan shell with a glossy white interior. Beaks small, approximately central. Hinge has about 20 prominent teeth.

A thin, elongated shell, rounded at the front end and with its hind end drawn out to a pointed, upturned tip.

Burrows into muddy sand or mud, especially in estuaries and bays, just below the low water mark and in shallow water. Nova Scotia to N. Carolina and Alaska to northern Calif.

Short Yoldia is similar in color but shorter, and has about 50 teeth in hinge; it grows up to 1½in long. Found from Arctic Ocean to N. Carolina in offshore waters. Comb Yoldia is olive-yellow with a yellow interior, about 12 teeth in the hinge and grows up to an inch long; it lives off both northern coasts.

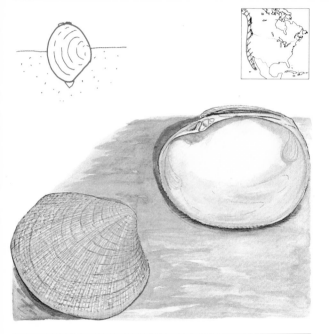

Creamy white to purple brown in color, often with brown zigzag markings. Strong axial ribs are crossed by small concentric ribs, closer together near the margin.

A strong, thick shell, longer than high. The beaks are at the front end, pointing forwards. Interior white. Edible and collected commercially.

In sand and sandy mud, from low tide level to shallow water. Aleutian Islands, Alaska to southern Baja Calif., most common north of San Francisco.

Thin-shelled Littleneck is flattened, with thin chalky valves; it is found in shallow water from Vancouver to Baja Calif., but is often washed onto beaches. **Smooth Washington Clam** (also known as Butter Clam) lives deep in sand, in bays and shallow water from Alaska to Calif., and makes good eating.

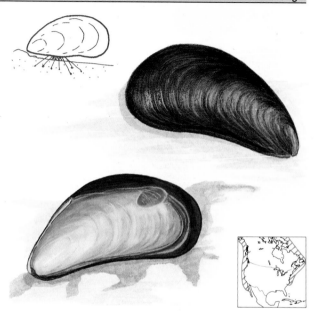

Blue-black in color with a shiny periostracum, eroded away in places. Smooth in texture with no ribs but with concentric growth lines.

A thin, elongated shell with the curled beaks at the front end. It has a smooth hinge, without teeth. The interior is pearly white with a deep blue border. Edible and eaten in large quantities, especially in Europe.

Attached by the byssus in large numbers, to rocks, pilings and wharves in the intertidal zone, near the low tide line. Arctic Ocean to S. Carolina and Alaska to Baja Calif.

Calif. Mussel grows up to 10in long; its thick shell has about 12 radial ribs and coarse growth lines. It is attached to intertidal rocks from Aleutian Islands to Mexico. **Black Musculus** has a brown-black periostracum and grows 2–3in long; it lives in shallow water off both northern coasts.

CLEAR JEWEL BOX

A white shell with many translucent, blade-like leafy projections. The right valve may be tinged with pink or orange.

An almost round, thick shell, with the beaks turned towards the right. The left valve (which is attached to the substrate) is large and more convex than the free right valve. The interior is opaque white. Edible.

Attached to pilings, breakwaters and stones from low tide level to water 250 feet deep. Free valves may be washed ashore. Oregon to Baja Calif.

Other jewel boxes occur on both coasts. Pacific Left-handed Jewel Box is an intertidal species which is attached by its right valve, so that its beak is turned towards the left. It has irregular scaly ridges. Leafy Jewel Box is attached to rocks in shallow water from N. Carolina to the West Indies.

PACIFIC PINK SCALLOP
W

2–3in

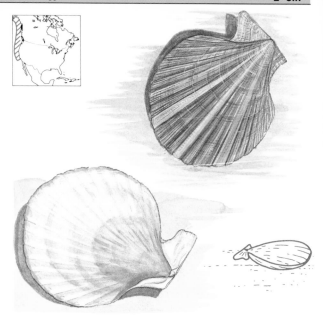

Color varies from pink to yellow or white; the color is often rayed or in concentric bands. There are 18–22 strong rounded ribs on each valve, with other fine scaly ribs between.

An almost round shell, with the hinge formed of unequal wings; the front wing is just over twice as long as the hind wing. Left valve is darker in color than the right valve. Shell is covered with sponges in life.

On sand, mud or rocks from low tide level into deep water. Scallops swim through the water by opening and closing the valves of their shells. Alaska to Newport Bay, Calif.

The similar Hind's Scallop lives on rocks from below low tide level to deep water, from Alaska to Calif. The edible Iceland Scallop lives in offshore waters on both northern coasts; it is dirty white and may be tinged red, with many rounded riblets and a front wing three times as long as the hind wing.

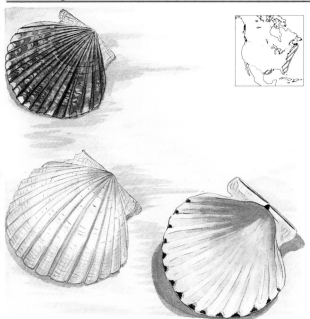

Banded with dark gray or brown, the color often following the 17–18 strong, rounded radial ribs. In many the lower valve is much lighter in color than upper one and may be almost white.

An almost round, inflated shell with the hinge formed of almost equal wings. A delicacy and caught commercially; but not as common as it once was, due to overfishing and to the disappearance of the eelgrass beds.

On muddy sand in shallow water, amongst eelgrasses. Nova Scotia to northern Florida and Texas.

Atlantic Deep Sea Scallop is the most important commercially. It is almost round, smooth, reddish in color. Giant Pacific Scallop is the edible Alaskan scallop that grows 6–8in long. Calico Scallop varies in color from rose-pink to mauve and yellow. It is found in shallow water from Maryland to Texas.

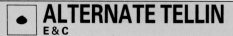
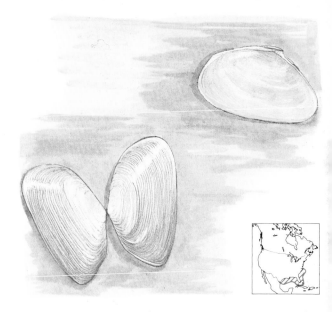

A large tellin, with a series of fine, evenly spaced concentric grooves on the outside of each valve.

A solid, elongated, compressed shell. It is glossy and variable in color, basically white often tinged with pink or yellow. Interior white, similarly tinged. The front end is rounded, the hind end is pointed and has a slight twist.

Lies buried on its left side in sand, with one siphon reaching to the surface of the sand and the other projecting above it. Shallow water to water 400 feet deep, N. Carolina to Texas.

Rose Petal Tellin is about 1½in long, has a strongly twisted hind end, and is white or flushed with reddish pink; occurs from Florida to Texas and West Indies. Taylor's Tellin, from Gulf states, is pink. Angulate Tellin is green-yellow with three yellow rays around beaks; occurs in Florida and Texas.

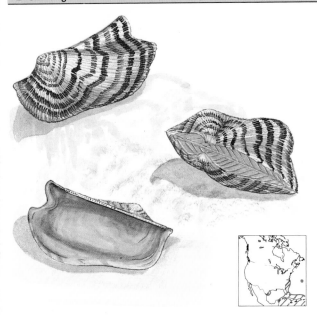

Distinctively shaped shell, yellowish-white in color with brown zigzag lines and strong ribs radiating outwards from the beaks. In life the shell has a thick brown periostracum.

A strong, inflated shell with a broad straight hinge interrupted by the beaks about a quarter of the way from the front end. The hinge has about 50 teeth. Used in shell craft and jewelry; edible and eaten in the West Indies.

Attached by its byssus to rocks and corals and in crevices, from low tide level to shallow water. N. Carolina to Florida, southern Texas, Bermuda and West Indies.

There are several other arks living on the east coast and in the Caribbean. Mossy Ark, which has the same range as the Turkey Wing, is similar in shape but has a much larger opening for the byssus on the ventral side. It is brown in color but lacks the zigzag stripes, and has beaded ribs.

97

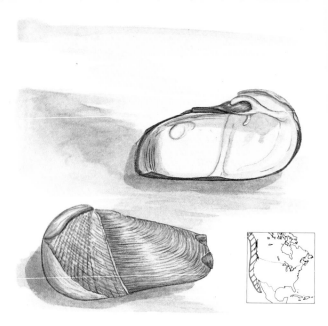

Front end of shell inflated, with many fine scaly ridges. Hind end more elongated, wrinkled in texture. The two parts are separated by an oblique groove.

Front end is closed by calcareous plates which curve over the margins in front of the beaks. The beaks are a quarter of the way along the shell from the front end, and there is a short stout "tooth" beneath each one.

Bores into soft rocks, wood and clay from low tide line to shallow water. Alaska to central Baja Calif.

The gray-white Scale-sided Piddock bores into clay and soft rocks in intertidal and shallow waters on the Calif. coast. It is similar to the Common Piddock, but grows up to 6in long and has a broad spoon-shaped "tooth" beneath each beak.

An irregular gray-white or brownish shell with a wrinkled exterior and rough concentric growth lines. Interior greenish-white. Muscle scar is same color as the rest of the interior.

The shape of the shell varies according to the position in which it grows. Right (bottom) valve is flatter than the left (upper) valve. Now superseded commercially by the Giant Pacific Oyster, but still harvested.

In oyster beds on mud flats, in brackish water of estuaries and bays and on rocks, near the low tide level. Southern Alaska to southern Baja Calif.

The Giant Pacific Oyster, introduced from Japan, has become the west coast commercial oyster. Similar to Eastern Oyster, it grows up to 12in long, has a whitish muscle scar and thick ridges on the shell. The dark purple or black Columbian Oyster lives attached to mangrove roots in Baja Calif.

A grayish-white thick shell with irregular, coarse radial ribs, obscured by wrinkled growth lines. There is a large opening near the top of the shell for the byssus.

A large, more or less round shell with a pearly white interior.

Attached to rocks, stones and pilings from low tide level to deep water. Alaska to Baja Calif. Single valves may be found on beaches.

Common Jingle Shell has a thin, strong, yellowish shell, up to 2in long, with an almost closed notch at the top for the byssus. It is attached to wharves, rocks, from Cape Cod to West Indies. Prickly Jingle Shell is smaller, wrinkled and pale gray; attached to rocks, wharves from Labrador to N. Carolina.

WHITE SAND MACOMA

2–4in long

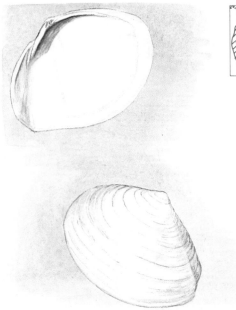

The largest western macoma. The left valve is almost flat, the right valve inflated. A large rib runs diagonally inside the shell, from just behind the hinge to the hind end.

A large ovate shell, with thin glossy valves, creamy exterior and white interior. The front end is rounded, the hind end short and truncated, and the shell is twisted to one side at the hind end. Makes good eating.

Lies buried horizontally in sand and sandy mud, with the left valve down. In beaches and bays from the intertidal zone into deep water. Vancouver Island to central Baja Calif.

All macomas have twisted hind ends. They are distinguished by details of muscle scars and lines inside shell. Baltic Macoma is white with a thin gray periostracum; it lives in intertidal and shallow waters on both northern coasts. Bent-nose Macoma (Alaska to Baja Calif.) lives beneath mud in quiet waters.

OCEAN QUAHOG OR BLACK CLAM

E

2–5in long

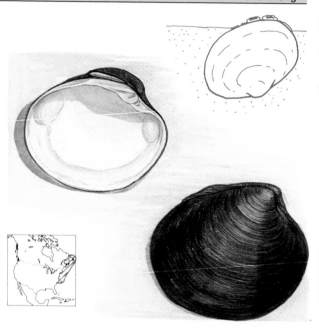

Almost circular in outline with concentric growth lines. Whitish with a thick brown periostracum. Interior white and chalky.

A large, thick-shelled, smooth and chalky bivalve. The large beaks are turned forwards and there is a heart-shaped depression in front of the beaks. An important clam and caught commercially in the northeast.

Burrows in sand in water 30 to 100 feet deep. Newfoundland to N. Carolina.

True **Quahogs** are gray-white and have no periostracum. They are found intertidally on eastern sandy beaches.

ATLANTIC THORNY OYSTER

2–5in long

E & C

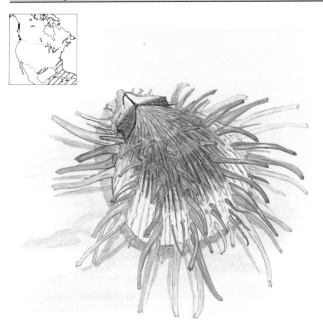

This shell has many long thin spines and the top valve has many spiny radial ribs. The color varies, from white with yellow or pink beaks to all pink or yellow.

A large, almost circular, thick shell with small "wings" on the hinge. The hinge is of two interlocking teeth, so well fitted together that the valves can only be separated halfway without damaging the teeth.

Attached to rocks, wrecks, sea walls, from shallow water to water 150 feet deep. N. Carolina to Florida, Texas and the West Indies. Worn shells may be found on Florida beaches.

Pacific Thorny Oyster is a heavy, thick shell which grows up to 5in long; it is pink or reddish in color with long blunt spines. It is found attached to rocks and wrecks in deep water in the Gulf of Calif. and worn valves may be found on beaches.

A large, heavy, irregularly thickened shell. Dirty gray exterior, white inside with purple muscle scar. Right valve of shell is flat, left valve convex and larger than the right.

Elongated in shape, narrow at the front and rounded at the back but varying in shape with the position in which it is growing. This is the common eastern edible oyster, commercially produced in large quantities.

On sand or mud in shallow water, especially in brackish conditions. Gulf of St Lawrence to Gulf of Mexico and West Indies.

The whitish Crested Oyster grows up to 3in long; it is found on rocks, pilings and buoys in salt water from low tide to shallow water, Maryland to the West Indies. The **Native Pacific Oyster**, from the west coast, lives on intertidal mud flats in bays and estuaries.

A mauve-gray shell with white beaks. The thick brown-black periostracum has long hairs.

A heavy, oval, inflated shell, smooth but for concentric growth lines and with the beaks near the narrow front end. The hind end is broadly rounded. Interior gray-white. Edible and eaten in Europe.

Amongst rocks and stones from below low tide line to deep water. From the Arctic Ocean to New Jersey in the east and to southern Calif. in the west. Often used as bait for fish.

False Tulip Shell is similar but only half the size; found in shallow water from N. Carolina to Caribbean. Fan-shaped Horse Mussel grows 4–6in long; has a thin, inflated shell with a two-tone periostracum, yellow-brown on hind two thirds, dark brown at front. It lives in shallow water from B.C. to Calif.

105

GIANT ATLANTIC COCKLE
E & C

Pale yellow with a red-brown band on back slope of shell and brown shading on the margin; it often has concentric rows of brown spots. It has about 35 strong, rounded radial ribs.

A strong, inflated shell with rounded beaks and serrated margins. Interior of shell pale red, white at the front. Edible and makes an excellent chowder.

Burrows into sand and mud, from below low tide level to water 100 feet deep. Often washed ashore. Virginia to northern Florida, Texas and Mexico.

East coast cockles include **Prickly Cockle**, gray white with a yellow or brown interior and prickly ribs; and **Yellow Cockle** with scaly ribs and a white interior. Iceland Cockle lives off both northern coasts; it has ridged radial ribs crossed by coarse growth lines. **Nuttall's Cockle** is eaten on west coast.

Shell grayish or whitish, tinged orange; inside white stained with purple. The shell has many concentric, rib-like growth lines but there is a smooth area in the center of each valve.

A large, solid, thick shell, more or less round and quite inflated, with prominent beaks. Used for chowders commercially and young clams are baked in their shells as "cherrystones." The purple-stained shells were used by the Indians as wampum.

Burrows in sand and mud in bays and inlets, from the intertidal zone into water 50 feet deep. Gulf of St Lawrence to Florida and Gulf of Mexico. Introduced to Humboldt Bay, Calif.

Southern Quahog is a heavier, more inflated shell without a smooth area in the center of the valves; its interior is white. It is found from southern N. Jersey to Texas, in shallow water.

3–6in long

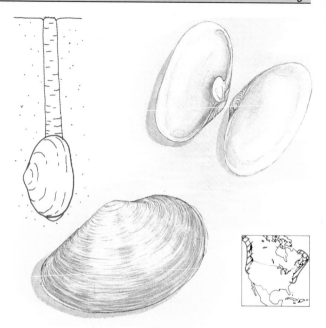

Grayish white, chalky shell with a thin brown periostracum.
Valves gape at both ends. There is a spoon-like "tooth" beneath
the beak in the left valve.

An ovate, thin-shelled bivalve with a rough texture and concentric
growth lines. This clam forms the basis for a large commercial
fishery but it is threatened by pollution and large intertidal
specimens are rare, due to intensive collection.

Burrows in sand and mud from intertidal zone into water 250 feet
deep. Labrador to N. Carolina. Introduced to the west coast from
Alaska to San Francisco Bay.

Truncate Softshell Clam grows up to 3in long; its hind end is
abruptly truncated. It lives in northern seas. **Geoduck** lives three
feet down in intertidal sand on the west coast. **Pacific Gaper** is
yellow-white with a gray periostracum; it lives in sand in shallow
water on the west coast.

PACIFIC RAZOR CLAM

W

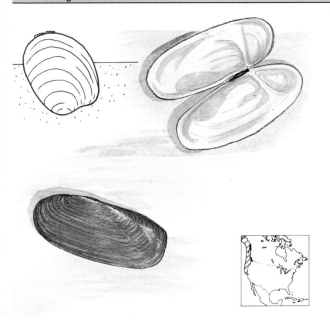

Oblong with rounded ends, flattened in cross section. Whitish gray, covered with a thin, shiny, olive green or brown periostracum. Valves gape at both ends.

Interior glossy white tinged with purple, with a distinct rib running from the top towards the front end. Hinge positioned about a third of the way along the shell from the front end. Edible, collected commercially in northern part of its range.

Burrows into sand and mud in the intertidal zone, especially near the low tide mark. Alaska to Monterey, Calif.

Atlantic Razor Clam is 2–2½in long. It is found in shallow water and on sand flats from the Gulf of St Lawrence to N. Carolina. Transparent Razor Clam burrows in sand at low tide on the coast of Calif. False Jackknife Clams, from both coasts, are more inflated with cylindrical shells.

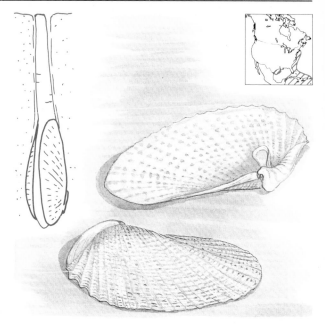

A pure white, elongated, winglike shell with many beaded ribs. The beaks are rolled over. Inside the shell, beneath the beak is a broad, spoon-like "tooth."

A large, thin, quite fragile shell with valves which gape widely. The beaks are found a quarter of the way along the shell from the front end. In life there are two accessory shells over the hinge.

Burrows into deep sandy mud at low tide level and in shallow water. South Massachusetts to Texas and the West Indies but rare in the north.

Fallen Angel Wing grows about 2in long; it bores into mud from Massachusetts to West Indies. Valves of Campeche Angel Wing are washed onto beaches from N. Carolina to West Indies. **False Angel Wing** resembles true angel wings but lacks the "tooth;" occurs from Prince Edward Island to Gulf of Mexico.

Yellow-white with a yellow-gray periostracum. The prominent beaks are positioned slightly to the front of center and point forwards.

A large, heavy shell, oval in shape and more or less smooth with irregular growth lines. Caught commercially and used in clambakes.

Beneath the surface of sand, mud or gravel from low tide level to 140 feet deep. Cast up on the shore in large numbers after winter storms. Nova Scotia to S. Carolina.

Other surf clams live off both coasts. Calif. Surf Clam has a thin white shell with a gray-brown periostracum. It lives in intertidal and shallow waters from Puget Sound southwards and is used for chowder. Stimpson's Surf Clam, white with a shiny yellow-brown periostracum, lives off both northern coasts.

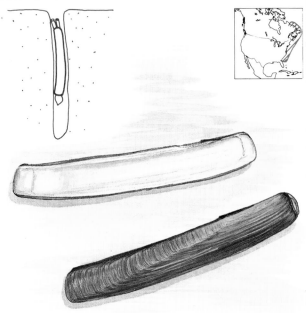

An elongated, curved shell with parallel sides and squared ends. Interior white, with a low flat ridge running from each beak to the front end.

A large whitish shell covered by an olive-green, shiny periostracum. The hinge is near the front end; it has two vertical teeth on the left valve, one on the right valve. Both ends of the shell gape widely.

Burrows in sand in the intertidal zone, especially near the low tide level. Labrador to S. Carolina.

The similar Minor Jackknife Clam grows up to 3in long; it lives in intertidal sand from New Jersey to Texas. Green Jackknife Clam is about 2in long, and is found from Rhode Island to the Gulf states. Blunt Jackknife Clam lives in sandy mud flats from B.C. to Baja Calif.; it grows from 2–4in long.

112

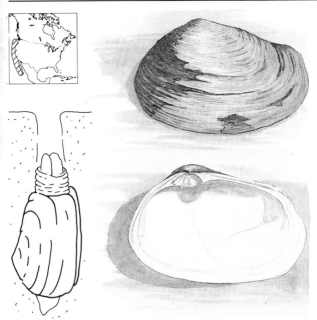

This shell is shaped like a rounded oval with a large gape at the hind end. The large beaks are found about a third of the way along the shell, from the front end.

A strong, smooth, quite inflated shell, yellow-white in color with a gray or brown periostracum. Collected and considered a delicacy in Calif. but not caught commercially.

Beneath the surface of the sand from low tide level to water 100 feet deep. Washington state to Baja Calif.

Alaskan Gaper or Horse Clam occurs in intertidal sand and mud from Alaska to Monterey, Calif. It is more oval, more inflated and grows up to 10in long. **Atlantic Surf Clam** and other surf clams are oval with a central beak.

113

GEODUCK

W

4–9in long

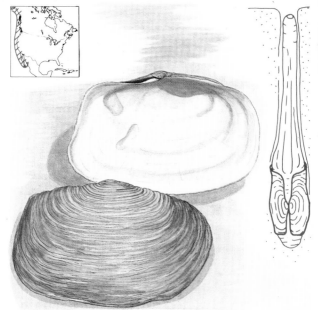

Hind end of the shell is squared off; the valves gape at both ends. Exterior has coarse, concentric wavy lines.

A large, thick, oblong shell. Gray-white with a thin brownish yellow periostracum. Interior white. Edible but difficult to collect.

Lives three feet down in mud, from the intertidal zone to shallow water. Alaska to central Baja Calif. In life this clam has a huge siphon that cannot be withdrawn into the shell.

Atlantic Geoduck is similar but uncommon, found from N. Carolina to Texas. It grows up to 5in long. **Pacific Gaper** and **Softshell Clam** are not truncated at the hind end.

Grayish-brown to black in color, with 15–20 radial ribs bearing hollow spines. The spines are larger towards the upper, rounded end. Mantle bright orange-gold in life.

A large, rather fragile, fan-shaped shell. The upper margin is straight and the lower one curved. Interior is gray-brown often mottled with dark orange; it has a large muscle scar at the front end which is partly surrounded by the pearly area.

Buried in sand and sandy mud, pointed end down and rounded end projecting above sand when tide is in. Low tide level to shallow water from N. Carolina to Florida and Caribbean.

Saw-toothed Pen Shell is common in shallow water off east coast; it is yellow-gray to brown with over 30 ribs bearing small, hollow, tooth-like spines. Dead shells are washed ashore with Stiff Pen Shells. Half-naked Pen Shell, from the east coast and Bahamas, is smaller with a pale yellow mantle.

115

OTHER SMALL BIVALVES

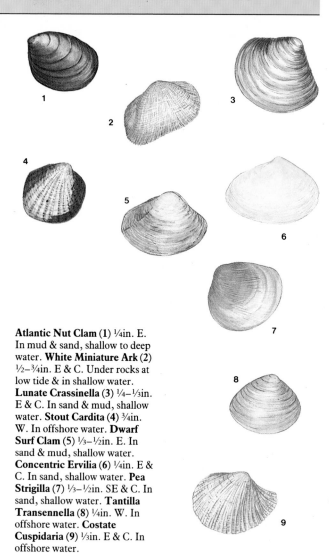

Atlantic Nut Clam (1) ¼in. E. In mud & sand, shallow to deep water. **White Miniature Ark (2)** ½–¾in. E & C. Under rocks at low tide & in shallow water. **Lunate Crassinella (3)** ¼–⅓in. E & C. In sand & mud, shallow water. **Stout Cardita (4)** ¾in. W. In offshore water. **Dwarf Surf Clam (5)** ⅓–½in. E. In sand & mud, shallow water. **Concentric Ervilia (6)** ¼in. E & C. In sand, shallow water. **Pea Strigilla (7)** ⅓–½in. SE & C. In sand, shallow water. **Tantilla Transennella (8)** ¼in. W. In offshore water. **Costate Cuspidaria (9)** ⅓in. E & C. In offshore water.

OTHER SMALL BIVALVES

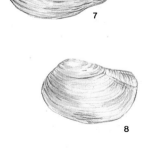

Miller's Nut Clam (1) ½–1in. E
& W. In sand & mud, offshore
water. **Kitten's Paw (2)** 1in. E &
C. On rocks & shells, intertidal
& shallow water. **Common
Atlantic Awning Clam (3)**
½–1in. E. In mud, shallow water.
Dwarf Tiger Lucine (4) ¾–1in.
E & C. In sand & mud, shallow
water. **Small False Donax (5)**
½–1in. SE, C & SW. In sand
in surf. **Lightning Venus (6)**
1–1½in. E & C. In mud & sand,
shallow water. **Calif. Cumingia
(7)** 1–1½in. SW. In crevices &
on pilings, intertidal to shallow
water. **Gould's Pandora (8)**
¾–1½in. NE. In mud & sand,
intertidal to deep water.
Unequal Spoon Clam (9)
½–1½in. SE & C. In sand,
shallow water.

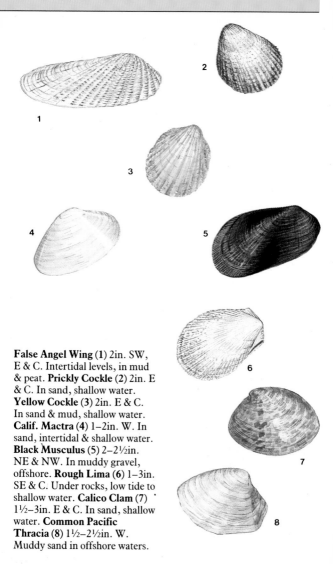

False Angel Wing (**1**) 2in. SW, E & C. Intertidal levels, in mud & peat. **Prickly Cockle** (**2**) 2in. E & C. In sand, shallow water. **Yellow Cockle** (**3**) 2in. E & C. In sand & mud, shallow water. **Calif. Mactra** (**4**) 1–2in. W. In sand, intertidal & shallow water. **Black Musculus** (**5**) 2–2½in. NE & NW. In muddy gravel, offshore. **Rough Lima** (**6**) 1–3in. SE & C. Under rocks, low tide to shallow water. **Calico Clam** (**7**) 1½–3in. E & C. In sand, shallow water. **Common Pacific Thracia** (**8**) 1½–2½in. W. Muddy sand in offshore waters.

OTHER BIVALVES

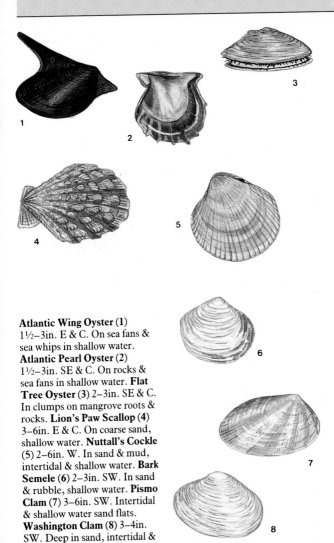

Atlantic Wing Oyster (1)
1½–3in. E & C. On sea fans & sea whips in shallow water.
Atlantic Pearl Oyster (2)
1½–3in. SE & C. On rocks & sea fans in shallow water. **Flat Tree Oyster (3)** 2–3in. SE & C. In clumps on mangrove roots & rocks. **Lion's Paw Scallop (4)** 3–6in. E & C. On coarse sand, shallow water. **Nuttall's Cockle (5)** 2–6in. W. In sand & mud, intertidal & shallow water. **Bark Semele (6)** 2–3in. SW. In sand & rubble, shallow water. **Pismo Clam (7)** 3–6in. SW. Intertidal & shallow water sand flats. **Washington Clam (8)** 3–4in. SW. Deep in sand, intertidal & shallow water.

CHITONS

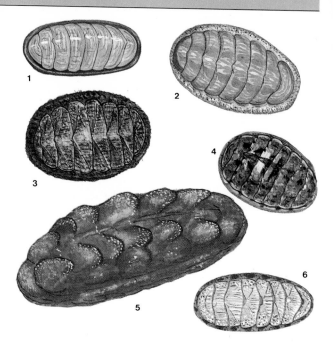

Chitons are flattened animals, elongated or rounded oval in shape. The shell consists of eight overlapping plates encircled by a girdle. Chitons live in the intertidal zone & in offshore waters, often in rock crevices or beneath rocks. They are found on all coasts but most species occur in the Pacific. They feed by scraping algae from the rocks. Northern Chitons are found on & under rocks on both coasts. **White Northern Chiton (1)** grows up to ½in long. It lives in intertidal & offshore waters.

Red Northern Chiton (2) grows ½–1in long. It is found from low tide into deep water. Western species include: **Hairy Mopalia (3)**, 1–2in long, which lives on & under intertidal rocks; **Gould's Baby Chiton (4)**, about ½in long, which lives on intertidal rocks; & **Giant Pacific Chiton (5)**, 6–14in long, which lives amongst rocks & seaweeds at low tide level. **Common Eastern Chiton (6)**, about ½in long, lives in shallow water from Massachusetts to Florida.

TUSK SHELLS

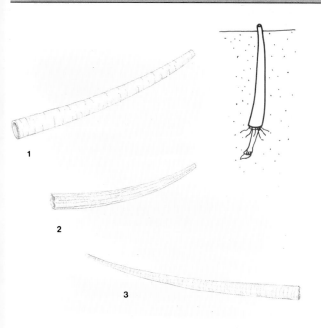

Mostly deep water molluscs. A few live in shallow water off both coasts. The shell is a simple tube, open at both ends. The tube is calcareous & tapered so that the opening at the front end is larger than the one at the hind end. Many are white, either smooth, with longitudinal ridges or with annular rings. They live buried in sand with the hind end projecting above the sand surface. They are filter feeders, drawing in a current of water & extracting small plants & animals from it.

The **Indian Money Tusk** (1) grows about 2in long. It is a west coast species that lives in offshore waters from shallow to deep water. These shells were dredged up by the coast Indians who valued them for decoration & as currency. **Six-sided Tusk** (2) comes from Calif. waters. It grows up to 1in long & has six strong ribs running the length of the shell. **Ivory Tusk** (3) comes from sandy shallow water, from N. Carolina to Texas & the West Indies; it grows 1–2½in long.

Index and check-list

All species in Roman type are illustrated.
Keep a record of your sightings by checking the boxes.

☐ Abalones	69	
☐ Black	69	
☐ Red	79	
☐ Alaba, Varicose	75	
☐ Alvania, Compact	74	
☐ Angel Wing	110	
☐ False	110, 118	
☐ Arene, Gem	74	
☐ *Arks*	97	
☐ White Miniature	116	
☐ Astartes	87	
☐ Boreal	87	
☐ Augers	50	
☐ Common American	50	
☐ Awning Clam, Common Atlantic	117	
☐ Barrel Bubbles	25	
☐ Western	25	
☐ Bittersweets	86	
☐ West Coast	86	
☐ Bittium, Giant Pacific Coast	76	
☐ Black Clam	102	
☐ Bleeding Tooth	36	
☐ Bonnets	56	
☐ Scotch	56	
☐ Bubbles, Adam's Baby	75	
☐ Barrel	25	
☐ Paper	26	
☐ Butter Clam	91, 119	
☐ Caecum, Beautiful	74	
☐ Calico Clam	118	
☐ Carditas	80	
☐ Carpenter's	80	
☐ Stout	116	
☐ Carrier Shells	55	
☐ Atlantic	55	
☐ Ceriths	40	
☐ Florida	40	
☐ *Chinese Hat, Pacific*	32	
☐ Chink Shells	15	
☐ Northern	15	
☐ Chitons	120	
☐ Cockles	106	
☐ Giant Atlantic	106	
☐ Nuttall's	106, 119	
☐ Prickly	106, 118	

☐ Yellow	106, 118	
☐ Colus, Stimpson's	79	
☐ Conchs	63	
☐ Crown	61	
☐ Florida Fighting	63	
☐ *Florida Horse*	64	
☐ Cone Shells	58	
☐ Alphabet	58	
☐ Mouse	78	
☐ Coquina Shell	83	
☐ Coral Shell, Short	78	
☐ Cowries	67	
☐ Atlantic Gray	77	
☐ Deer	67	
☐ Crassinella, Lunate	116	
☐ Crown Conchs	61	
☐ Common	61	
☐ Cumingia, Calif.	117	
☐ Cup-and-saucers	32	
☐ Striated	32	
☐ Cuspidaria, Costate	116	
☐ Diplodons	85	
☐ Pacific Orb	85	
☐ Distorsio, Atlantic	78	
☐ Dogwhelks	19	
☐ Common Eastern	19	
☐ Dogwinkles	48	
☐ File	48	
☐ *Donaxes*	83	
☐ Small False	117	
☐ Dove Shells	20	
☐ Greedy	20	
☐ Lunar	75	
☐ Drillias	17	
☐ White-knobbed	17	
☐ Dwarf Olives	33	
☐ Purple	33	
☐ Dwarf Tritons	22, 27	
☐ Carpenter's	22	
☐ Ervilia, Concentric	116	
☐ Fig Shell, Common	79	
☐ Flamingo Tongue	42	
☐ *McGinty's*	42	
☐ Fossarus, Fenestrate	75	
☐ Frog Shell, Calif.	79	

☐ Gapers		113
☐ Pacific		113
☐ Geoduck		114
☐ *Atlantic*		114
☐ Hairy Shells		21
☐ Boreal		21
☐ Helmets		72
☐ Queen		72
☐ Hoof Shells		18
☐ White		18
☐ Horn Shell, Calif.		78
☐ *Horse Clam*		113
☐ Horse Mussels		105
☐ Northern		105
☐ Jackknife Clams		112
☐ Atlantic		112
☐ *False*		111
☐ Jewel Boxes		93
☐ Clear		93
☐ Jingle Shells		100
☐ False Pacific		100
☐ Junonia		70
☐ Kellias		84
☐ La Perouse's		84
☐ Keyhole Limpets		45
☐ Little		45
☐ Kitten's Paw		117
☐ *Lacuna, One-banded*		15
☐ Latirus, Chestnut		78
☐ Lima, Rough		118
☐ Limpets		35, 46
☐ False		77
☐ Fingered		35
☐ Keyhole		45
☐ Plate		46
☐ Littlenecks		91
☐ Common Pacific		91
☐ Loras		23
☐ Harp		23
☐ Lucines		89
☐ Buttercup		89
☐ Dwarf Tiger		117
☐ Lyonsias		81
☐ Glassy		81
☐ Macomas		101
☐ White Sand		101
☐ Macron, Livid		77
☐ Mactra, Calif.		118
☐ Margin Shells		14
☐ Common Atlantic		14
☐ Margarite, Striated		76
☐ Melanella, Carpenter's		75
☐ Miters		37
☐ Beaded		37
☐ Modulus, Atlantic		77
☐ Moon Shells		65
☐ Lewis'		65
☐ *Milk*		54
☐ Mopalia, Hairy		120
☐ Murexes		53, 62
☐ Apple		62
☐ Festive		78
☐ Florida Lace		53
☐ Pitted		62, 77
☐ Thorn Drupe		78
☐ Musculus, Black		92, 118
☐ Mussels		92
☐ Blue		92
☐ Horse		105
☐ *Nassas*		19, 39
☐ *Naticas*		54
☐ Livid		76
☐ Neptunes		68
☐ Common Northwest		68
☐ *Nerites*		36
☐ Virgin		76
☐ Nut Clam, Atlantic		116
☐ Miller's		117
☐ Nutmegs		49
☐ Common		49
☐ Odostome, Fine-sculptured		75
☐ Olives		52
☐ Dwarf		33
☐ Lettered		52
☐ *Rice*		33
☐ Oyster Drill		27
☐ Oysters		99, 104
☐ Atlantic Pearl		119
☐ Atlantic Wing		119
☐ Eastern		104
☐ Flat Tree		119
☐ Native Pacific		99
☐ Thorny		103
☐ Pandora, Gould's		117
☐ Paper Bubbles		26
☐ Gould's		26
☐ Pelican's Foot		51
☐ Pen Shells		115
☐ Stiff		115
☐ Periwinkles		28
☐ Beaded		77

123

☐	Common	28
☐	Northern Yellow	28, 76
☐	Pheasant Shell, Spotted	74
☐	Piddocks	98
☐	Common	98
☐	Pismo Clam	119
☐	Planaxis, Atlantic	75
☐	Plate Limpets	46
☐	Puncturella, Hooded	45, 77
☐	Purple Snails	38
☐	Common	38
☐	Pyram, Adam's	76
☐	Quahog, Northern	107
☐	*Southern*	107
☐	Ocean	102
☐	Razor Clams	109
☐	Pacific	109
☐	Risso, Catesby's	74
☐	Rock Shells	57
☐	Florida	57
☐	*Japanese*	22
☐	Sayella, Brown	75
☐	Scallops	94, 95
☐	Atlantic Bay	95
☐	Lion's Paw	119
☐	Pacific Pink	94
☐	Semele, Bark	119
☐	Shark Eye	54
☐	Simnia, Common West Indian	76
☐	Slipper Shells	44
☐	Atlantic	44
☐	Softshell Clam	108
☐	*Truncate*	108
☐	Solarielle, Channeled	74
☐	Spindle Shells	66
☐	Coue's	66
☐	Spoon Clam, Unequal	117
☐	Star Shell, *Green*	43
☐	Long-spined	78
☐	Stomatella, Painted False	74
☐	Strigilla, Pea	116
☐	Sundials	47
☐	Atlantic	47
☐	Surf Clams	111
☐	Atlantic	111
☐	Dwarf	116
☐	Tellins	82, 96
☐	Alternate	96
☐	Salmon	82
☐	*Sunrise*	83
☐	Thorn Drupe	78

☐	Thorny Oyster, Atlantic	103
☐	*Pacific*	103
☐	Thracia, Common Pacific	118
☐	Top Shells	29, 41
☐	Black	41
☐	Western Ribbed	29
☐	Transennella, Tantilla	116
☐	Tree Oyster, Flat	119
☐	Trifora, Black-lined	75
☐	Tritons	59
☐	Dwarf	22, 27
☐	Hairy	59
☐	Trivias	24
☐	Coffee Bean	24
☐	Tulip Shells (gastropods)	64
☐	Banded	64
☐	Tulip Shell, False (bivalves)	105
☐	Tun, Atlantic Partridge	79
☐	Turbans	43
☐	Carpenter's Dwarf	74
☐	Chestnut	43
☐	Turbonilles	16
☐	Vancouver	16
☐	Turkey Wing	97
☐	Turret Shells	31
☐	Boring	31
☐	*Turrids*	66
☐	Tusk Shells	121
☐	Vase, Caribbean	79
☐	Venus, Lightning	117
☐	Vitrinella, Suppressed	74
☐	*Volutes*	70
☐	Music	79
☐	Washington Clam	91, 119
☐	Wedge Clams	88
☐	Arctic	88
☐	Wentletraps	30, 34
☐	Angulate	30
☐	Wroblewski's	34
☐	Whelks	39, 60, 71
☐	Channeled	71
☐	Common Northern	60
☐	Dire	39
☐	Wing Oyster, Atlantic	119
☐	Winkle, Common Prickly	76
☐	False Prickly	77
☐	Worm Shells	73
☐	Variable	73
☐	West Indian	79
☐	Yoldias	90
☐	File	90